LIFE HACKS
(Preparing Yourself for Life)

A Practical Guide for Success Written for
Teenagers and Young Adults

By Robert S. Roussey

DORRANCE
PUBLISHING CO
EST. 1920
PITTSBURGH, PENNSYLVANIA 15238

Dorrance Publishing Co
585 Alpha Drive
Suite 103
Pittsburgh, PA 15238
Visit our website at *www. dorrancebookstore.com*

ISBN: 979-8-88729-425-4
eISBN: 979-8-88729-925-9

LIFE HACKS:
My tips, suggestions, and ideas to help you in Preparing Yourself for Life

Chapters 1 to 7 –
These chapters provide tips on how to get you into the work force –
hopefully into your dream job

Chapters 8 to 19 –
At this point in the book you are now employed –
these chapters provide tips on how to succeed in your job or profession
and in life, all the way through to retirement

PREFACE

At the age of fourteen, I decided that I would focus on accounting and auditing as my life and career goal. Shortly after my fifteenth birthday, I received a part-time job as an assistant bookkeeper in a builders' hardware company and worked for six years for that enterprise during my high school and college years. Upon graduating from college, I was employed by an international public accounting firm and worked for thirty-five years until my retirement as a worldwide partner in the firm. Upon retirement, I received six offers from colleges and universities around the country, and accepted a full-time offer as a Professor of Accounting in the clinical (i.e., a scholar from practice) faculty of one of the top universities in the country, where I worked for another twenty-two years. This work experience amounted to a total of sixty-three years of traveling the world; participating in the development of a global accounting firm; participating in the development of professional accounting and auditing standards in the United States; participating in the development of these standards for the International Accounting and Auditing Profession; participating in the development of audit, control, security, management, and governance over information technology in the United States and globally; and participating in the ethical accounting education of over fifteen hundred students in the Master of Accounting program at the university.

While I was always thankful for receiving that first job in accounting at age fifteen, it was only during my professorship years that I realized how truly fortunate I was to have focused on a career at age fourteen. The students in the Master of Accounting program had all started studying economics, marketing, communication, humanities, science, liberal arts, and other majors. What I heard from these students was either they ended up not liking their choices, were unable to get a job in the field they had chosen, or they wanted to get a master's degree in a completely different field.

Upon retirement from the university, I have had the opportunity to speak with numerous teenagers who have been floundering about what they want to do with their lives. How, as a teenager or young adult, should one focus on life, on a job, on a career, on skill development, or on becoming part of the Fourth Industrial Revolution, and how can one succeed? This became the genesis for this book, to not only help these young people to prepare themselves for a working life, but also on how to become successful in life, all the way through to retirement.

I decided to write this book based on my own experiences and my interactions with people around the world, particularly with young people. I have included personal examples from my own life to reinforce the messages in each of the chapters of the book. My CV (Curriculum Vitae) is included in Appendix A.

CHAPTERS

CHAPTER 1

THINKING ABOUT WHAT YOU WANT TO DO WITH YOUR LIFE

Principle: *"The earlier you start thinking about your future, the earlier you can create your future."*

Have you ever thought seriously about what you want to do with your life? If you have not, perhaps you should give it a try! It is never too early, or too late, to do so.

Try dreaming or thinking about your future just before you go to sleep. The more you dream or think about ideas for your future, the earlier your dream or your ideas will become more focused. As you focus more on your future, those dreams or ideas become clearer and clearer. As the dreams or ideas start to shape a future life, you can then start to contemplate how you might achieve that life. The earlier you think about your future, however, the better your future can become a reality based on your dreams, your ideas, and your thoughts.

Do you dream about becoming a skier, a snowboarder, a boxer, a lawyer, an accountant, a doctor or surgeon, a nurse, an engineer, a computer scientist, an entrepreneur, a mathematician, a sportsperson, a comedian, a Hollywood Star, a dancer, a financier, a banker, an airline pilot, a salesperson, a horse trainer or a jockey, a mechanic, serving in the military, a psychiatrist, a paralegal, a designer, an artist, or any one of hundreds of other jobs or professional aspirations?

The earlier in life you can set a dream, the easier it will be to achieve the dream.

So, do try to set that DREAM as soon as you can.

Try setting a dream on something that you would enjoy doing for a thirty-five-,forty-five-, fifty-five--year period. Remember, if you love doing something, it will be a joy to go into work every day.

If you love your job, it will not be work, but it will become a life endeavor and it will be FUN! The only problem is that the years will go by very fast, and because of that fast passage of time, you must remember to be good to your friends and family and to have fun every day as you go through life.

But in setting that dream, LOOK TO THE FUTURE!

Look five, ten, fifteen years or more into the future to determine what job or professional position will be in great demand in our changing, future economy.

You do not want to select a job or professional position in a dying business or industry. Instead, you want to consider those jobs or professional positions that will CREATE THE FUTURE of our society.

We are in what some are calling the Fourth Industrial Revolution. This revolution is based on the ever-changing use of technology and science. It is creating new jobs and new avenues for success and, at the same time, eliminating other jobs.

This is your time to seize the moment, take risks, and become part of this "Revolution."

Before we leave this chapter, however, let me discuss the aspects of a dream, dreaming, thinking, focusing, or imagining. In the context of this book, all these terms are somewhat similar.

For example, according to yourdictionary.com,

> "The definition of a dream is an image, thought or fantasy that happens in the mind while a person is sleeping or relaxing."

According to google.com, a dream

> "Is to experience dreams during sleep, or to indulge in daydreams or fantasies about something greatly desired."

In other words, you can dream about something of importance to you while you are relaxing, or you can daydream about something of importance to you. Or you can "focus" on something of importance to you. This dreaming or focusing can be on something that is of immediate importance to you, or can be on something that is of future importance.

Here is an example of something of immediate importance and future importance, in the words of Bertrand-Gabriel Vigouroux, a French winemaker:

> "My high-quality wines start in my dreams and mind. The common characteristics
> are always around balance, drinkability and expression of the purity of the grape."

In this simple quote, the winemaker is dreaming about the future of making good wines and is focusing on the immediate characteristics of what makes high-quality wines.

Putting the winemaker's dreams in the context of this chapter, you need to dream (think, focus, imagine) about your future, and then start to dream (think, focus, imagine) how you can make that dream a reality.

Personal Example

My father died with I was fourteen years old. My mentor was gone. I had to focus on and decide what to do with my life. In other words, I had to dream or focus on something of importance to me. I thought I might like to go into a profession, such as a becoming a lawyer, a doctor, or an accountant. Since the first two professions required extra education, I put them out of my mind and tried to focus on becoming an accountant. Also, I needed to get a job to help support my family (my older brother had been called into the Air Force for the Korean Conflict), and to save money for my future education. I was fortunate because when I told my high school track coach that I could no long run track, he was able to get me a job at his friend's company as an assistant bookkeeper. I worked in that company all through high school and college and ended up being promoted from an assistant bookkeeper to an assistant bidder on construction projects, such as the New York Coliseum, to becoming the assistant to the President. Upon graduation from college, I did get a job in the accounting profession, where I worked for thirty-five years until my retirement.

CHAPTER 2

FOCUSING ON EDUCATION

Principle: *"Make education a fun part of your life"*

Whether you are in grade school, high school, trade school or college, this is the time to concentrate on education in developing your skill set(s) for the career of your dreams. Think of your education as a precursor to your life career.

Focus on those subjects that will provide you with a rounded education and on the subjects that will enable you to develop the skills needed for your possible chosen career.

Work with your guidance counselor to help you set up the classes that will get you to your goals.

Your education can be viewed from several perspectives: (1) Having fun, (2) Creating life-long friendships, and (3) Learning and developing skills.

Having FUN!

Creating life-long friendships

Learning and developing skills.

(1) Having FUN!

There is nothing wrong with having fun in grade school, high school, and college. Some of you friends might not like this, but fun is not drinking in high school, excessive drinking in college, or getting HIGH on whatever!

Both drinking and getting high are forms of escape from the norm of reality. Both can become addictive and can ruin your life.

What is fun? It can be:
- enjoying life in a lively, lighthearted way,
- hanging out with friends/family,
- making new friends,
- watching your team win (or lose) at a football or basketball game,
- going on a date for the first time,
- walking across a beautiful campus,
- riding a chair lift in Colorado or the Swiss Alps and seeing the beauty of nature,
- skiing the slopes,
- going to that special dance,
- hiking the High Peaks in the Adirondack Mountains,
- skateboarding,
- hang gliding,
- sailing,
- going to a great concert,
- having a great discussion on politics/sports/science,
- traveling in foreign lands,
- making a great presentation in class,
- how you make your job interesting and fun, and

• anything YOU WANT TO MAKE IT, as long as it brings a smile to your face or to your disposition and for you to feel good in a lively and lighthearted way.

But what do I mean by making education a fun part of your life? The typical education cycle of a person in the United States can range from about twelve to sixteen years. If you do not make your education cycle a fun part of your life, then you may be wasting a significant part of your life.

Can school be fun? Yes, if you make it fun! Be positive in your thinking about school. Be positive in your learning about the basic core subjects in school. Pay attention and be engaged in your classes, be involved in your classes, and participate in the learning process. Look at each subject as if each one is the most important subject of the day. Each class and each subject provide you with skills that become the basic set of skills that become the building blocks of life-long learning.

Personal Example

In grade school, I focused on my schoolwork, basketball, playing stickball in the streets of Brooklyn, and being an altar boy. My school had a basketball team, and we were in the Catholic Youth Organization (CYO) league. We played against other teams in the CYO, traveling around the city to play against other teams. We even played at Madison Square Garden in New York City. I was captain of our team, and it was my first experience in a leadership position. Thinking back, this was one of the ways I had FUN. Playing a game, I liked, playing with the other boys on the team, who were my friends, traveling around the city, and learning what it meant to be a leader. But most of all, it was hanging out with my friends, one of whom became my best friend, who went on to high school with me, and became one of my life-long friends.

Was going to grade school FUN? To an extent, it must have been! I enjoyed learning, getting good report cards, and being one of two graduates to get a scholarship to high school. My focus on having fun continued through high school and through my college years.

(2) Creating life-long friendships

Campus Life. The time you spend in school is a great period of your life to get involved in the campus activities outside of class and to meet new people who could become life-long friends.

Shared Interests. The sharing of interests of members of a sports team, a computer club, a chess club, or other activities that may be of interest to you is a great way to meet and to develop friendships.

Personal Example

In college, I was part of a group of ten guys and gals who hung out together between classes and who went to all the sporting events, dances, bars, and other functions together.

(3) Learning and developing skills

Whether you are in a high school, a trade school, a junior college, or a college or university, is there a better place to learn a multitude of subjects that will provide you with a good education? Probably not! What a great time it is to focus on learning and developing skills for the future. All the formal educational process becomes the bedrock of the foundation for your life-long learning process.

But what is a good education?

Education can be defined somewhat as the process of facilitating learning, or the acquisition of knowledge, skills, values, beliefs, and habits. Educational methods can include storytelling, discussion, teaching, training, directed research, and <u>participation</u> by the student in the educational process.

In the modern world we live in today, the educational process needs to include the traditional subjects of math, history, science, literature, psychology, etc., to provide a well-rounded mindset, but also the subjects for the jobs of today and tomorrow.

Surgeons of fifteen years ago marvel at the advances in medicine after their retirement. The accountants and auditors of yesteryear who labored over paper worksheets are astounded by the processing of transactions that become lost in the memories of the computer systems and the cloud environment.

If you considered any of the jobs/positions mentioned in chapter one, you need to look for schooling that will not only give you a good liberal arts background but will also have the courses needed to start your development of the skill sets needed to achieve your dreams/goals in life.

Participation in Your Education

Education is not a one-way street coming from the educator to the student. It should be a two-way thoroughfare with interaction between the educator and the student,

When possible and practical, get to know your teachers, instructors, professors, and others who could help you in developing skill sets and who could become mentors. Also, see how you can interact with your classmates, see how you could learn from others either in a structured or unstructured environment, and see how you could become a mentor to others.

Personal Example

In my high school, the curriculums were such that you could either focus on liberal arts courses, or on a split between liberal arts and business-type courses. I chose the latter because I did want to get a well-rounded education having both liberal art classes and classes in business, such as bookkeeping and accounting. (The business classes included a course on "typing." Who would have thought that twenty-five to thirty years later typing would be so useful in the developing microcomputer age?) The bookkeeping and accounting courses not only helped me in my new job as an assistant bookkeeper but also prepared me for my college classes.

While in high school, I did develop some life-long friends, participated in my education, while working twenty-six hours a week in a builders' hardware company in New York City. My high school also had a student council, and I was on one of three teams running for the student council in my junior year. Our team did not win, but it was another great experience of being involved in the school process; in learning about the focus of a student council for the betterment of students and teachers, in the learning process, as well as learning about the election process itself.

CHAPTER 3

FOCUSING ON SOCIAL ACTIVITY AND ON PHYSICAL ACTIVITY

Principle: *"Focusing on Social Activity and on Physical Activity can prepare you for appropriate interaction with your peers and for a healthy body."*

SOCIAL ACTIVITY

Social Activity can be considered to be a broad category of ways to communicate with others by the sharing of ideas through spoken words, or through words in a written text, or through cartoons, or through symbols (such as an emoji), or by playing games online, or by just "hanging out" with friends or colleagues and discussing the issues of the day or what is happening in our lives.

Social Activity can also be considered to include interaction on social media sites on the internet. These social media sites can be very useful in the exchanging or sharing of data and information. These sites can also be very useful for business activities and for individuals who become "influencers" for products or for the dissemination of concepts or ideas.

No matter how Social Activity may be defined or considered, all of the above aspects of Social Activity are important for the development of our minds and how we can communicate with others. In my mind, all of the above aspects are important for such development.

But also keep in focus the broad aspect of such communications where **balance** between all of the ways to communicate is critical to full development of Social Activity. Try to participate in all such activities and try not to focus on only one or two of them. If you only focus on playing games or on the internet aspects of social media, you are missing out on the physical interaction with others.

The physical interaction with other persons is so important in developing confidence in the verbal or written expression of our thoughts and ideas as a young person. Talking face-to-face with our friends, presenting verbal reports in school, and writing essays are all important parts of the physical Social Activity development that can lead you to future confidence, happiness, and success.

PHYSICAL ACTIVITY

What can one say about Physical Activity and diet, except to say that they are **important**!

Physical Activity does not mean sitting on a couch and moving fingers on a keyboard. It does mean moving around, walking, running, lifting weights, playing soccer, baseball, basketball, or studying karate or a number of other similar activities.

Physical Activity combined with a good diet makes mind and body strong and hopefully more able to stay healthy and stave off illness and disease.

CHAPTER 4

WHAT REALLY EXCITES YOU OR WHAT MAYBE WILL INTEREST YOU

Principle: *"Focusing on a job or on a profession you may like may lead you to a job you will want to do every day of your working life."*

You join an extracurricular activity at school involving making robots and entering competitions with other schools to see who can make the most inventive, interesting, and useful robot. You get involved in developing ideas for robots; presenting arguments to back up your ideas; developing designs for robots and how they might be used in future applications in business, in teaching, in manufacturing in space exploration and in other workforce areas; developing engineering designs for them; and in determining how to use software and other technologies to make them work most efficiently. Suddenly, you become excited about the possibilities and start to focus your education on engineering, software development, and computer applications. In effect, you get excited about something that really interests you and creates an educational environment that can lead to a challenging, interesting, and fun career.

Or, at a young age, you think about becoming a horse trainer. Maybe it is because you have been around racing tracks all your life and you have found you have a gift with animals. Sometimes this does lead to becoming a horse trainer. Or your love for animals may lead you to the field of animal husbandry.

Maybe at a young age you had to take care of a sister/brother, an elderly parent or relative and the experience helped you in developing a set of skills in helping others. Such an experience could be the basis for you to focus on a career in helping others via careers in nursing, teaching, medicine, medical research, psychology, and so many other related fields.

Perhaps at an early age you find that you are a gifted athlete. You get involved with some of the athletic programs at school and find that you not only excel at the sport but that you love it as well. Many of the world's famous athletes got their start in school athletic programs. However, you must be realistic about your chances of achieving success in the sport, and you should get the counsel of parents, athletic directors, and, most of all your, coaches.

As previously mentioned, the earlier you can find a focus in life, the earlier you can start to work toward your goals through education, personal study, internships, and part-time and full-time work experiences.

In finding a focus in life, another aspect is to consider whether you want a job or a job within a profession. The difference between the two can depend on the level of skills you can develop or the amount of education you desire or can afford.

For example, getting a job might be defined as obtaining a

position and being paid for the work you do as part of regular employment, such as a worker in the retail industry, a groundskeeper at a golf club, an elevator technician, a service technician at a car dealership, a lift engineer at a ski resort, and similar jobs.

Getting a job within a profession might be defined as a job that requires extensive education in a particular field, and that requires adhering to the technical and ethical standards of the profession, such as the law, medicine, or engineering. There are also other fields of endeavor using the term professional that requires a completely different set of skills and education, such as a professional golfer or a professional football player.

The next two chapters focus on skills and on getting skills through education, and may help to clear your focus on jobs or jobs within a profession.

Personal Example

Or, like I did, you decide on a profession/career and focus on it all through high school and college, and then get an opportunity to get a job and follow that job through retirement. Did I know when I decided to become an accountant that it would really excite me or even be of interest to me? No, I did not! But my decision to focus early on a career did get me into a profession that was interesting, challenging, ethical, educational, and financially rewarding. In addition, the professional work motivated me, provided me with the opportunity to be a volunteer, provided me with the opportunity to become part of a worldwide profession, and, yes, provided me with the opportunity to have great FUN as I went through thirty-five years in the profession.

CHAPTER 5

DEVELOPING A SKILL SET

Principle: "Focusing on a specialized skill within a broad range of skills will create a well-rounded person capable of making a difference in life."

What is a skill set? According to Webster's New World College Dictionary, skill can be defined as:

1) Great ability or proficiency; expertise that comes from training and practice.

2) (a) An art, craft or science, especially one that involves the use of hands or body; and

(b) an ability in such an art, craft or science.

3) Knowledge, understanding, or judgement.

In other words, a set of skills that may set you apart and allows you to "**MAKE A DIFFERENCE**" in your life as compared to others.

For example, let us assume that all your life you liked to make things or design things. Perhaps it started with Lego sets and you first made the sets designed by Lego, but then you started to use the Lego pieces to design your own creations. As you moved through your early years, you saw other things you would like to have and started designing how you might make or build these things. Whether the "things" were a treehouse, a skateboard ramp, a design of a new skateboard, or developing that "robot" mentioned earlier, the consideration of designing or making such things could lead you to becoming proficient as a designer or as an engineer. If so, you might want to become "skilled" as a designer or engineer and lead you to a study of such crafts though YouTube, through "online" courses, through high-school courses or university courses that will give you the skills to help "MAKE A DIFFERENCE" in your life, or to set you on a path to achieve some goals that you have set for yourself.

Some of these skills developed early in life can be used as building blocks to create an expertise in an area, subject, or science that in future years will set you apart from your peers.

If these skills excite you at some point in your life, you may then want to expand and develop those and other skills further: in more formal education at high school; through a working on-the-job training program; at a community college; or at a college level.

Dreams vs. Reality

While I truly believe that we need to follow our dreams (remember chapter one?) or a job or profession that excites you, sometimes there is a need for a reality check, i.e., a practicality check.

What do I mean by a reality or practicality check? I guess it means that before deciding to focus on your "dream" skill, you need to consider whether that skill will provide you with an "employable skill."

For example, if your dream skill is to be an elevator operator, you need to determine if there is a current need for elevator operators. Generally, there was a need for such operators in the 1940s and

1950s, but since all elevators are computerized today, there is no longer a need for such operators anymore, i.e., this is a dead profession. Similarly, what if your dream skill is to become a historian? In such a case, you should do some research to determine the current and future need for historians.

Sometimes, you may not have a dream and that is okay also. However, I do suggest that you look at something you may want to do in life and, at least, start in that direction. You may find that going in that direction will lead you a position that becomes a "life position," and it may even lead you to your "dream job."

In today's environment, perhaps, you need to not only consider your dream skill but also to consider what are the needs for skill sets of the future.

So, what are some of the future skill sets?

According to the SHRM "Skills Gap Study," there are five main skills that will be essential to succeed. These are

- Technology and computer skills,
- Digital literacy and competency,
- Working knowledge of tech-enabled tools and techniques,
- Robot and automation programming, and
- Critical thinking

According to Crimson Education in South Africa, and other studies, students can future-proof their careers with **"STEM"** qualifications in

- **Science**
- **Technology**
- **Engineering**
- **Mathematics**

According to Bernard Marr, an internationally best-selling author, popular keynote speaker, futurist, and a strategic business and technology advisor to governments and companies, the Ten Vital Skills you will need for the future of work are

1. Creativity
Human workers in the future will need to be creative to fully realize the benefits of all the new things for the future—new products, ways of working, and technologies.

2. Emotional intelligence (EQ)
A person's ability to be aware of, control, and express their own emotions as well as being cognizant of the emotions of others describes their emotional intelligence. You exhibit high emotional intelligence if you have empathy, integrity, and work well with others.

3. Analytical (critical) thinking
A person with critical thinking skills can suggest innovative solutions and ideas, solve complex problems using reasoning and logic, and evaluate arguments.

4. Active learning with a growth mindset
Anyone in the future of work needs to actively learn and grow. A person with a growth mindset understands that their abilities and intelligence can be developed, and they know their effort to build skills will result in higher achievement. They will, therefore, take on challenges, learn from mistakes, and actively seek new knowledge.

5. Judgment and decision-making

Human decision-making will become more complex in the future workplace. As technology takes away more menial and mundane tasks, it will leave humans to do more higher-level decision-making.

6. Interpersonal communication skills

The ability to exchange information and meaning between people will be a vital skill during the fourth industrial revolution. This means people should hone their ability to communicate effectively with other human beings so that they are able to say the right things, using the right tone of voice and body language, in order to bring their messages across.

7. Leadership skills

Traits you commonly associate with leadership, such as being inspiring and helping others, become the best versions of themselves will be necessary for the future workforce.

8. Diversity and cultural intelligence

As our world and workplaces become more diverse and open, it is vital that individuals have the skills to understand, respect, and work with others despite differences in race, culture, language, age, gender, sexual orientation, political, or religious beliefs.

9. Technology skills

The fourth industrial revolution is fueled by technological innovations such as artificial intelligence, big data, virtual reality, blockchains, and more. This means that everyone will need a certain level of comfort around technology.

10. Embracing change

Due to the speed of change in the future workplace, people will have to be agile and able to embrace and celebrate change.

While a number of the skills described above have been critical in achieving our current state of business, the economy, and technology, the ten skills described above will be even more critical in developing the future economy, described by some as the "Fourth Industrial Revolution."

****

If you study closely the few skills described in this "Dreams vs. Realty" section, you will see that such skills are exciting, the forefront of future knowledge, and are, truly, the skills that "dreams are made of."

I invite you to "Dream Further."

Personal Example

In the job that I had all through high school and college, I developed several skill sets:

a) How to take direction in the performance of tasks, such as bookkeeping,

b) How to read blueprints in preparing bids for builders' hardware contracts,

c) How to think logically,

d) How to discuss financing with banks,

e) How to understand business operations, and

f) How to engage with follow workers.

In addition, at age seventeen, I learned downhill **skiing**, which I have now been doing for about sixty-seven years. This skill has provided me with the opportunity to ski around the world, meet follow ski enthusiasts, and, also, to develop life-long ski friends.

As my career developed, I focused on leadership, critical thinking, creativity, technology, future needs, judgement, decision-making, entrepreneurship, and how to apply those skills in helping my firm grow revenue from a twenty-two-million-dollars-a-year firm to a revenue of $6.7 billion a year when I retired after thirty-five years. I will describe some of these matters in later chapters.

CHAPTER 6

APPLYING THAT SKILL SET IN EDUCATION

Principle: *"Look to developing skills in formal and informal educational settings."*

If you now have a skill set that you would like to pursue further, now what do you do? A lot depends on your personal motivation, your focus in life, and what you can and cannot afford.

PURSUE IT YOURSELF

There are many self-made people in this world who have taken an idea, developed the idea into a business, and developed specific skills during the process.

Perhaps the most notable example is Mark Zuckerberg, who took the idea of social contact at the university level and brought it to the world. How many skills did he have to develop in order to achieve this feat? Probably quite a few skills, from understanding computers, developing a social interaction platform, marketing, creating a business, taking the business public through the securities market, becoming a businessman, and becoming a chief executive officer. Did he do it alone? Probably not without the help of others who had skill sets he did not have at the time. I am sure he had to rely on others in developing his skill sets during the process of creating FACEBOOK (now known as "Meta").

PURSUE IT THROUGH SELF-STUDY COURSES

There are many self-help books, self-study courses, and online training courses that will assist you in developing a skill set or skill sets.

For example:

The Price of Tuition – Is the Desire to Learn, by Charles D. Hayes

The Science of Self-Learning: How to Teach Yourself Anything, Learn More in Less Time, and Direct Your Own Education (Learning How to Learn Book 1) by Peter Hollins

The Study Skills Handbook (Macmillan Study Skills) eBook by Stella Cottrell

Skills for Success: Personal Development and Employability by Stella Cottrell

Small Acts of Leadership by G. Shawn Hunter

While there are many, many more such books and courses, however, the key to the use of such material is, as Charles D. Hayes so aptly put, "Is the Desire to Learn."

PURSUE IT THROUGH ON-THE-JOB TRAINING

This topic of self-development is as old as the craft guilds of the eighteenth and nineteenth centuries of Europe to the current "intern" positions.

In many countries in the European Union today, companies employ the use of this so-called "on-the-job" training for those prospective employees who do not have the finances or desire to attend a university or college program to develop skills to succeed in life.

Many companies in the United States have such programs, and I can see a future where such companies will have to expand these programs to acquire the employees needed to achieve their business objectives and plans.

PURSUE IT THROUGH COMMUNITY COLLEGES

If the above discussion does not appeal to you, maybe you should focus on developing skills at a community college.

These colleges provide an opportunity to focus on specific skills such as Business and Information Technology, Health Sciences and Wellness, Math and Science, Liberal Arts, Communication and Design, Manufacturing, Social Sciences, Education, general education courses, or focus on the courses designed to provide you with the course background for the first two years of a university program. This latter background generally means that you would be able to apply to a university for the last two years (junior and senior) with the ability to transfer the community college credits for the first two years of its curriculum and for that university to accept those credits.

Community colleges are, generally, more local, provide an education at a lower cost, provide day, night, online, and summer courses, all to fit the needs of its students. The class sizes are, generally, small, diverse, and include a variety of ages and backgrounds.

PURSUE IT THROUGH THE MILITARY

Another group of "entities" that employ "on-the-job" training are the military forces in the United States, as well as other countries around the world. Such training not only provides skill development in various fields but also provides discipline, respect, and the need to follow orders. In addition, there are some military programs that provide funding for college or university education after a period of service in the military.

Some of the ways you can get the military to pay for part of your skill development are

1) Paying for College. The military offers many educational benefits for service members to afford and further their education during or after service, such as financial aid, college funds, and loan repayment programs.

2) Military Schools. These schools, such as service academies, senior military colleges, and maritime academies, offer world-class education in exchange for a period of service commitment.

3) The ROTC Program. The Reserve Officer Training Corps is a paid college program that prepares young adults to become officers in the US military in exchange for a commitment to serve in the military for a period of time after graduation.

PURSUE IT AT THE COLLEGE OR AT THE UNIVERSITIY LEVEL

While the terms college and university are often used interchangeably, both terms refer to schooling at the postsecondary level. The term college generally refers to an institution that offers undergraduate or associate degrees. The term university usually means a large institution that offers graduate and doctorate programs in addition to undergraduate degrees.

While a college degree does not guarantee success, and college is not for everyone, it is for some. According to Statista, in 2018, there were about 19.65 million students in public and private colleges in the United States, and Statista projects the number of students will reach 20.11 million by the year 2029.

Attending a college or a university, however, is not inexpensive, and the cost of such an education should be taken into consideration. If you can afford it, are able to get scholarship funding, or can work to pay for some of the cost of this level of education, then it should be put into the mix of educational considerations. *One word of caution, however, is to think very carefully about going to a college or university and end up with a significant amount of student loans or debt that will be difficult to pay in later years.*

Nonetheless, at colleges and universities across the United States, and in other countries, a student can pursue the development of skills for many, many jobs and professions.

Do you want to be a writer, a historian, an educator, a researcher, an economist, a doctor, a nurse, a dentist, an entrepreneur, a scientist, a computer scientist, an accountant, a marketing expert, a dancer, an organizational expert, an engineer, a pilot, a production expert, a communication specialist, an environmental expert, a financial advisor, or any one of a multitude of other jobs/professions? There is a college or university that will provide the courses to develop and expand the skills necessary for you to be ready to enter into the world of business, non-profits, or governments.

All you need to do is focus on a skill/expert area and find a college or a university that will be a good fit for you.

Personal Example

In high school, I continued to focus on accounting and thus developed my skill level in bookkeeping and accounting. In looking to further develop my accounting skills, I looked at colleges and universities that had a well-recognized accounting program, and that had a connection with the accounting firms for on-campus interviews and job placements. I found such a university in New York City, and I was able to attend classes in the mornings and work in the afternoons at the builders' hardware company to pay for my tuition.

Once I completed my "formal" education, I read self-help books, engaged in self-study of topics and concepts, participated in firm training programs both as a student and teacher, was amazed at the firm's on-the-job training programs, and continued to build a number of other skills as part of my skills education foundation.

CHAPTER 7

FOCUSING ON A WORK ETHIC FOR YOUR JOB OR ON A PROFESSION

Principle: *"A work ethic will lead to success in life."*

The Work Ethic Principle

Now that you have some basic job skills, I believe it is important to think about the "work ethic" concept or principle.

One of the great benefits of living in a country like the United States of America is the focus of a government designed to serve and protect its people, and the focus of business to innovate for the creation of new products and services for its people, its consumers, and its investors. This combination of government and business has created a great economic model allowing citizens to work, innovate, and to create good lives for themselves and their families. This combination has also developed a strong work ethic among the people of this country.

This work ethic principle has been around for centuries, and together with immigration, education, opportunity to work, fostering racial integration, family development, capitalism, industrial and consumer development, this principle has created an economic engine in the United States of America that benefits its people and other people around the world.

In my mind, a person either has or needs to develop a work ethic in order to succeed. Thus, before starting to consider a job or a profession, you need to think about your work ethic.

Do you have it because of summer employment, because of working in a fast-food chain as a teenager, working on a golf course during the summer, or working in the ski industry during a winter break?

If so, you probably know the value of working and the value of doing a good job for your company/boss and doing a good job for the customers in your workplace.

If you did not have such an experience, then you need to ask yourself, "Do I have what it takes to be an employee who will help my employer/company succeed and who will provide good services to our customers?" If you answer "yes," then you have focused on another skill that will set you up for success.

Let us discuss for a moment this concept of the work ethic. It can be described as

"A principle that hard work is intrinsically virtuous or worthy of reward."

Generally, many scholars have considered that there are ten work ethic traits: appearance, attendance, attitude, character, communication, cooperation, organizational skills, productivity, respect, and teamwork.

For example, Georgia Piedmont Technical College instructs and evaluates students on work ethics in all programs of study in designated courses in each of the academic schools, excluding arts and sciences. The ten work ethic traits, are defined as essential for student success and are described further below. The definition of each of these traits has been integrated into the program courses of each program curriculum, thereby allowing each program to make work ethics a relevant and meaningful part of the program curriculum.

1. Appearance: Displays proper dress, grooming, hygiene, and manners.

2. Attendance: Attends class, arrives and leaves on time, tells instructor in advance of planned absences, and makes up assignment promptly.

3. Attitude: Shows a positive attitude, appears confident, and has true hopes of self.

4. Character: Displays loyalty, honesty, dependability, reliability, initiative, and self-control.

5. Communication: Displays proper verbal and non-verbal skills and listens.

6. Cooperation: Displays leadership skills; properly handles criticism, conflicts, and stress; maintains proper relationships with peers and follows chain of command.

7. Organizational Skill: Shows skills in management, prioritizing, and dealing with change.

8. Productivity: Follows safety practices, conserves resources, and follows instructions.

9. Respect: Deals properly with diversity, shows understanding and tolerance.

10. Teamwork: Respects rights of others, is a team worker, is helpful, is confident, displays a customer service attitude, and seeks continuous learning.

Thus, Georgia Piedmont Tech strives to ensure a strong culture of work ethic that is the focus for both staff and students. The promotion of proper classroom and on-the-job conduct is the duty of all. Courses reinforce the work ethics traits through discussion, modeling of conduct, and in homework. Instructors continually include the work ethics traits informally throughout the program courses.

While your skill development period may not have had such a rigorous program as Georgia Piedmont Tech, you can be sure that your employer will be evaluating you on such traits in addition to the specific skills needed for your employment.

"Clervism.com" has a website that provides good examples of demonstrating your work ethic to your employer.

Job or Profession

When you get to a point where you believe your personal traits and skills now make you employable, it is time for you to start considering where and how your skills can get you an employable position. What do you need to consider?

Dream Job

Start with remembering your dream of a dream job. Don't give up the dream but do use the dream to help you focus further on what you can do for the near future or, even, for the rest of your life. However, you do need, as discussed earlier, to **temper** your dream job with the concept of **practicality**.

For example, a person who loves surfing may not be able to finance a surfing career but may be able to further his dream and create a fulfilling career by working in the surfing industry. Further, by working in the surfing industry, that person may become the designer of the future surfboard, or the marketer of surfboards, or the salesman traveling around the world selling surfboards, or become an executive of the surfboard company, or become an entrepreneur by setting up his/her own surfboard company.

Sometimes, the alternative does turn into the "dream job" of a lifetime.

Research

Perform some research to look at industries/companies/area of the country where jobs are available for people with your skill level. Perform research on an industry or industries and then perform research on companies in the industry or industries.

Connections

Another focus is to discuss with family, friends, others with any connection to an industry or companies in an industry, or others who work in the industry of interest to you. Such discussions are often an early way to get an interview or to get you connected with people who might be able to get you an interview.

Job Fairs

What are job fairs? A practical description can be:

A job fair, also referred commonly as a career fair or career expo, is an event in which employers, recruiters, and schools give information to potential employees. **Wikipedia**

However, many job fairs not only provide information about jobs but also provide the opportunity for employers to find employees. These are good sources to consider for potential employment.

Recruiting Websites

There are recruiting websites that provide a central location for businesses to find potential employees. These websites enable candidates to review position opportunities and to provide their resume and application information directly to potential employers.

On-Campus Recruiting

A very important resource for students at community college and at colleges and universities around the country is the on-campus recruiting process. This process marries the institution with the employer to enable a recruiter to visit the institution's campus to start an employment process with the institution's students. Some of these institutions of higher learning have also started to set up "virtual" interview process with companies that are not able to visit their campuses.

In some situations, the process may start off hiring students in intern positions that might lead to full-time positions after the internship period. Other times, the process is designed to hire students for full-time employment.

Either way, this is an excellent way to get a job or to enter a professional organization.

Personal Example

As mentioned earlier, my track coach got me a job while in high school, where I worked at that job until I graduated from university. I developed a work ethic at this job because I liked the work, the people, the industry, and I worked twenty-six hours a week after class and forty-four hours a week during the summer.

I was also fortunate because my university had an on-campus

recruiting process. I was interviewed on campus and then invited to firms for further interviews. I was also fortunate to be hired by an accounting firm that became my dream job.

CHAPTER 8

GETTING TO KNOW YOUR JOB OR YOUR PROFESSION

Principle: *"The more you know, the more you can achieve."*

Okay. Let's say that you now have a job. What do you need to do to succeed in that job?
Here are a few things that you may want to consider:

<u>Become an Expert in Your Position</u>

This is now your opportunity to start a career. Start it by learning as much as possible about your position.

- Be attentive to instructions by your supervisor.
- Take notes – if not possible during the day, then write notes about any instructions given to you at night.
- Be punctual. Get in early to set yourself up for the day.
- Do not be a nine-to-five employee. Work late if necessary.
- Understand your job description and work to meet and exceed what is expected of you. If there are manuals about your position, study those manuals.

- If there are other employees in a position like yours, watch and learn from them if possible.
- Try to emulate the best of the best of your colleagues and try to become the best of the best.
- In today's "work-at-home" environment, you may be asked or required to work at home. If so, be sure to create a work ethic for your work at home job as you would if you were working in an office, factory, or traveling in an on-the-road job.

Sometimes, the first job can be boring. Regardless, this should not stop you from becoming an expert in that position. For example, if you are a first-year accountant/auditor and you find the audit steps to be repetitive and somewhat boring, then see if you can learn more about the area being tested, perhaps seeing if adjustments could be made to the audit tests, or seeing if you could make recommendations about the tests or area being tested that might benefit your firm or the company being audited. Looking at the work in a positive manner versus a negative manner will be better for you and for your own development.

Learn About Other Positions

If there are lateral positions that might be of interest to you, or there are positions above your level that require a promotion, then do similar research to learn about them. In other words, get to know the jobs around you that might be of interest after you become an expert in your first position.

Know Your Company

As you settle into your job, start thinking about the organization employing you, and where you fit within the organizational structure of the business, non-profit, educational, or government agency. If you are employed by a small business or a new start-up entity, the organizational structure might be very simple to understand. However, in a large entity it might not be so simple.

For example, if you are employed by a "public" company, meaning a company that has offered securities in the public financial markets, then that public company must file various documents with the Securities and Exchange Commission, an arm of the United States Government. In this case, you can easily access a document, such as a 10-K annual filing, that provides information on the business of the company, its risks, environmental matters, its officers and directors, including its financial statements and other significant information. This can give you a deep understanding of the company with a little extra effort on your part.

What if the entity is not a public company and is what might be called a "private" company, meaning a company that is owned by one or more individuals, or is a partnership, meaning an entity that is owned by a number of individuals that are "partners" in the entity. In this case, getting information on the entity might be a little more difficult to obtain. Nonetheless, you might find that the entity has manuals about the organization, its business, its Code of Conduct, its business practices and procedures, as well as its organizational structure that it has created for use in controlling the business and its employees. Also, the entity might have a website for use in attracting business, customers, and future employees that will provide you with valuable information on the entity.

Know Your Industry

If you have a job in a company that is in an industry, such as banking, manufacturing, oil and gas, pharmaceuticals, hospitals and health care, entertainment, airlines, investment banking, accounting and auditing, legal, insurance, or any one of a multitude of industries, then you need to get an understanding of the industry and its competitors.

Why? Because you want or should want to become a leader in your job, your company, and your industry! This is your future; you need to go for it!

Know How You Will Be Evaluated

Most business and governmental entities have an evaluation process. This evaluation process is normally designed to determine how its employees are performing, and is often the basis for promotions, salary increases, and termination. The process can be internal, within the company, i.e., evaluation/performance criteria that a supervisor uses to evaluate performance, or, in certain companies, it might include an external evaluation by customers or others who evaluate your performance through internet/smartphone queries.

As a new employee, for example, **why** do you "need to know how you will be evaluated"?

The very simple **answer: your future depends on your need to know!**

If you know or can find out about the various criteria others will use to evaluate your performance, then you can focus on that criteria as you are performing your work. If you focus on such criteria and make sure that your performance meets or, hopefully, exceeds the evaluation criteria, then you will be in a great position when the evaluation is completed by the supervisor.

Many times, an evaluation may include some "needs to improve" recommendations. Take these recommendations seriously and think about how you can perform better for your next evaluation.

Personal Example

As a new accountant/auditor, my first assignment was to be on the audit team auditing a brewery. In addition, the brewery was a public entity, and it was an out-of-town assignment. As a first-year auditor, I was a low person on the audit team, but it did not stop me from learning as much as possible about the company. On my own time, at night, I studied the company manuals, its 10-K filings, and as many other documents about the company and its industry that I could find. My focus was to get an understanding about the business of the company, its products, its operations, the brewing process, its customers, and its place in the industry. In addition, I did have to "sample" the various products.

As I applied audit steps to each part of the business, such as revenue and accounts receivable, I made sure that I understood how it fit into the business process and how it fit into the financial statements, upon which my firm would, at the end of the audit process, provide an auditor's opinion on the overall financial position and results of operations of the company.

Surprising to me, at the end of my four months in auditing the brewery, I knew more about the company than most of the people working at the company, except for the top management. I knew the learning experience I was applying was the right thing to do, and I employed the process on all my audits.

As to knowing your industry, my firm was in the public accounting profession. In my first year with my firm, I joined the New York State CPA Candidates Society as a member. After the first year as a member, I was asked to become the Treasurer of the Society, and after another year I was asked to become the President of the Society. As President, I made speeches to the full New York State CPA Society and gave progress reports on the activities of our Candidates Society to the Board of Directors of the NYS CPA Society. For a young CPA candidate, this was a great learning process. Several years later, as a new young manager in my firm, I was nominated to the New York State CPA Society's "Auditing Standards and Procedures Committee." Another great way to learn about my profession.

As to my firm's evaluation process, the firm did have a very vigorous process. In my first year with the firm, I did not understand the importance of understanding the criteria on which I would be evaluated. I was very fortunate that my work ethic and my focus on understanding the businesses of the entities being audited helped me to perform at a high level, which was reflected in my performance reviews.

However, once I got an understanding of the performance review process at my firm, I made sure that I got an understanding of the evaluation criteria, which actually helped me further in thinking about how I could perform at an even higher level.

CHAPTER 9

BALANCING WORK AND FAMILY LIFE

Principle: *"Quality time at work and with family can lead to happiness."*

As a single person, it is not too difficult to find a balance between working and your personal life. Working long hours, studying, traveling, spending time away from home can help in developing a career and in advancing a career. It is also a great time to be with friends and to further develop friendships.

This period is also a great time to develop the work ethic mentioned earlier and to reflect on what you need to do in the near-term future to be successful in your work and in your life.

This includes reflecting on dating, marriage, relationships, family, children, and where you think you want to be in the near future.

This includes how hard do you want to work to become the department manager, the supervisor, the chief designer, the head of engineering, the chief financial officer, the executive vice president, the chief executive officer, or the managing partner. To achieve any such positions or similar positions does take hard work, long hours, travel, and other personal sacrifices.

I have seen a number of people who have focused on success, at times, without focusing on relationships and family.

Nonetheless, when thinking about relationships and family, it is also important to consider how to **balance work and family life**. What does this mean? **To me it means how hard do you work to succeed in your work but, at the same time, how hard do you work to succeed in your relationships, in your marriage, and in raising your children.**

Getting the appropriate balance is critical in achieving success in life!

Personal Example

Perhaps the best way to discuss this balancing act is through some personal examples.

As a youngster, even though we did not have much money, my father would take the family for a month's vacation to a rental lake house in Connecticut, or to a beach house on the Connecticut side of Long Island Sound. I learned to swim, to fish, and took long walks with my dad, and those memories were very important to me, particularly after my dad died.

When I started at the accounting firm, I had a strong desire to succeed. I worked hard, traveled extensively, and studied for the Certified Public Accountants examination. I also looked to see how I could participate in the growth of the firm. At the same time, I was getting married, and my future wife and I decided it would be a great way to start our marriage by transferring to an overseas office. The firm had just opened an office in Tokyo, Japan, and we elected to transfer to that office. We spent five years in Japan. I worked six and a half days a week, often to two or three in the mornings. The office doubled its revenue every year. I studied for the Japanese CPA license, passed the test, and I am now a licensed CPA in Japan for life.

My wife got a job in a Japanese trading firm, learned Japanese, Ikebana (Japanese flower arranging), Sumi painting, the Japanese tea ceremony, had two children, and then did volunteering nurse work at the US army and naval bases during the Vietnam War. It was an incredible experience and we both felt, with all the hard work, that it was also a five-year honeymoon.

After returning to New York from Japan, I became the partner in charge of several international clients. It became clear to me that I would be working very hard on these clients and traveling the world extensively.

I remembered my childhood and told my wife about the wonderful summer experiences I experienced as a child. We decided to look for a house on a lake. Eventually, we found a camp being built on a lot next to my brother's camp in the Adirondack Mountains in New York State. It did not have running water or electricity, but it did have a wood burning stove and an outhouse. The house came with several acres of land and over one hundred feet of lakefront, with a price tag of ten thousand dollars. This became our home away from home where we spent weekends, with my wife and two boys spending the entire summer. This gave us a place to swim, to canoe, to hike, to teach the family how to sail, to play chess, bridge, and to hang out with each other. This truly became our home away from home and it is our family home to this day, which now has electricity, functioning baths, a well, and a heating system.

The Adirondack home and family vacations created an

opportunity for me to create the work/family life balance that, to me, is so important to success. This was reinforced in a conversation with my oldest son during a telephone call we had while I was in Singapore on a Monday before Thanksgiving. When my son got on the line, I mentioned to him that I might not be able to get back to the United States for Thanksgiving. At fourteen years old, he said something to the effect: "Dad, don't worry about it. We have always had such quality time as a family that missing a Thanksgiving dinner is no big deal. I will watch the family for you."

This thought from my son reinforced my view about **the importance of balancing your work and family life**.

While you might not be able to find a lakefront home as I did in creating the work/life balance, I would recommend that you consider how you can get a great work/life balance for you and your family. This could be through camping, family vacations, canoe trips, hiking, skiing, road trips, participation in the Boy Scouts and Girl Scouts, gaming, and other similar activities. The key point is to spend **quality time** with your family and friends.

CHAPTER 10

GETTING INTO SAVING

Principle: *"Savings can help in times of distress and can help in creating financial stability."*

Very few young people have an understanding about financial matters such as savings, budgeting, investing, mortgages, and pensions. Financial matters do require time and effort to learn about these topics, and time and effort to put some of them into practice. This book is not a financial planning guide, but there are a few topics that are important as you start to plan out your life. These matters can provide you with some tools for a sound financial future or, by ignoring them, can provide you with a lifetime of trying to adequately provide for your family and for retirement.

Savings

Several decades ago, the United States of America had a very low rate of savings. In recent studies, for example, the Organization for Economic Development (OECD) has placed the United States in the twelfth place among the countries with the highest rates of savings of disposable income in 2020, with a savings rate of 6.88 percent.

This does not mean that every person or family unit has a

savings rate of 6.88 percent. Based on other studies and general information available to the public, it does mean that some persons and family units save at a much higher rate, and most persons and family units save at a much lower rate or have no savings AT ALL.

One of my favorite mottos is "CASH IN KING." I have always believed in saving and have long advocated that persons and family units need to have cash savings of at least six-months to cover all known expenses. If you lose a job or there is a pandemic, you will have at least a six-month cushion to help you through unforeseen crises.

So, if you have little or no savings, then one of the first financial matters to consider is the simple act of saving. According to the Merriam-Webster dictionary, "saving, in economics, is the amount that is left after spending."

In its simplest form, saving is basically cash left over after all expenses. It can be cash that you receive as a gift from family or others for a special occasion. It can be the extra money you might earn (income) from doing odd jobs around your neighborhood or at a fast-food chain. If you do not spend that cash, then it is available for **savings**.

Not spending is a discipline that is not easy! In our consumer society, there are so many companies encouraging you to spend your money on clothes, tech gadgets, smartphones, vacations, and on and on. If you spend all your excess cash, then you will not have anything left over for **savings**. Thus, you need to develop a focus on how you spend your cash. This does require a discipline about not spending all your cash and a discipline (i.e., budgeting) about putting some of your cash away for your future.

One of the first things to do, if you have not done it already, is to open a savings account at your local bank or credit union and start saving for your future. If you are too young to open a savings account, ask your parents or guardian to open one for you. It is never too early to start saving, and it is never too early to start budgeting and creating a discipline of saving.

Budgeting

According to "Dictionary.com" budgeting "is an estimate, often itemized, of expected income and expense for a given period in the future, a plan of operations based on such an estimate, an itemized allotment of funds time, etc., for a given period."

This is a reasonable way to plan your life for a future period and to estimate your income and expenses to determine what your disposable income might be during that period. A simple way to create a budget is to us a spreadsheet, like Excel, to itemize your income and expenses. An example, is shown below:

	Jan	Feb	Mar	Apr	May	June	Jul	Aug	Sept	Oct	Nov	Dec	Total
Income													
Deduct Expenses:													
xxxxx													
xxxxx													
xxxxx													
xxxxx													
Disposable Income													
Savings													
Investments													

I will talk about saving for retirement in a later chapter; however, once you start saving, you should think about investing.

Personal Example

I started saving in my junior year in high school. These savings helped me to support my family, pay for my college tuition, and allowed me to buy a used car after I started my university years.

CHAPTER 11

STARTING AN INVESTMENT CLUB AND INVESTING ON YOUR OWN

Principle: *"Learning about investing and investing early can help in creating financial independence."*

How do you learn about investing? As mentioned earlier, you can learn by self-study, by taking classes, and by studying with others. A fun way to learn is to form an investment club with friends or work colleagues.

<u>What is an investment club?</u>

According to "Investopedia," "An **investment club** comprises a group of people who pool their money to make **investments**. Usually, **investment clubs** are organized as partnerships and after the members study different investments, the group decides to buy or sell based on a majority vote of the members."

It is relatively easy to start an investment club. There are many sites on the internet providing you with information on how to start such a club. One such site is www.betterinvesting.org, a non-profit organization designed to help members learn about investing and provides information on how to start a club.

Investing on Your Own

When you have enough cash resources and a good credit line, you may want to start building an investment portfolio of stocks and a limited amount of bonds. This will provide you with a way to focus on national and global markets and will start you on the road to wealth creation.

Wealth Creation

Thinking about wealth creation should start in your early twenties and should continue onto your retirement. Some ideas about planning strategies and money matters are

Planning strategies

- Prepare a "net worth" statement (Assets less Liabilities equals net worth)
- Insert your net worth on a spreadsheet and periodically update the spreadsheet with your changes in net worth
- Prepare a budget for the next year
- Prepare a plan for your strategies regarding income, cost of living expenses, entertainment, savings, and investments and consider any appropriate "Money Matters" discussed below
- Plan to "live below your means" – i.e., expected cash inflows should exceed your expected cash outflows
- Update your budget

Money Matters
- Eliminate any credit card debt on which interest is being charged
- Only use credit cards if you can pay off the balance monthly
- Save six (6) months cash as soon as feasible to cover expenses and other required cash out flows in the event of sudden economic change
- Start a savings regime:
  - Cash for investments
  - Cash for children's college education
  - Cash for retirement
- Start an investment program:
  - As an individual – stocks and a limited amount of bonds
  - With a group of friends – as an investment club or as partners
- Rent until you can afford to consider real estate
- Start considering real estate:
  - As an individual, or as a family ownership of a condo or a home
  - As rental property:
    - >As an individual, or
    - >With a group of friends
- Maintain enough term life insurance to protect your family
- Individual Retirement Account sponsored by employer
  - To the extent possible – invest the maximum to receive the maximum employer matching
  - When feasible – invest the maximum amount to obtain the before tax benefit

— When feasible — invest the maximum amount to obtain any after tax benefit of the tax deferral of income from the investment
- Keep debt to an absolute minimum
- Purchase low mileage used cars versus new cars
- Be conservative in your investment and cost of living strategies

Personal Example

I started two investment clubs: one in the first year after joining my accounting firm, and the second one after being recalled into the US Army during the Berlin Crises. In the first club, we had twenty accountants, all with about an equal knowledge of business and investing. It was a great learning experience. In the second club, we had about twenty soldiers from all walks of life and with a varying knowledge of business and investing. It also was a great learning and teaching experience. We did not make a lot of money, but the camaraderie was part of my personal idea of "creating wealth" among friends.

I started a real estate partnership with three of my best friends, but it could not get off the ground because two of us were recalled to active military service during the Berlin Crises.

A little later in life, I started to invest in real estate, first with the purchase (and mortgage) of a home for my family after we returned to the United States from Japan. I continued to invest in real estate through the purchase of rental condominiums (together with mortgages). Later, together with other Limited Partners, I started to invest as a Limited Partner in larger real estate projects managed by a General Partner.

My personal investment goals were to hold a certain amount in cash (remember: Cash Is King), and a balance of excess disposable income invested in a personal securities portfolio, in real estate and in retirement funds.

CHAPTER 12

BECOMING A VOLUNTEER

Principle: ***"Help others and help yourself by volunteering."***

VOLUNTEERING

Volunteering is not for everyone. But it might be something you may want to consider. Well, what is a volunteer? According to the Merriam-Webster dictionary, a volunteer is

"a person who voluntarily undertakes or expresses a willingness to undertake a service: such as: (a) one who enters into military service voluntarily. (b) one who renders a service or takes part in a transaction while having no legal concern or interest."

I personally like a simpler definition, such as

"A person who freely offers to take part in an enterprise or undertake a task."

Why might you want to consider, at some point in time, to be a volunteer: Here are several thoughts on volunteering that involve helping others, meeting other people, and helping yourself through membership in job-related or professional-related organizations.

Helping Others

This might be an altruistic goal of yours: meaning to have an unselfless concern for the well-being of others. Many people volunteer to help in food kitchens, in hospitals, in libraries, in retirement homes, in civic organizations, in charities, and in so many other worthy organizations.

Meeting Other People

If you are new to a community, becoming a volunteer to an organization of interest to you might lead you to meet other like-minded people.

Job-Related or Professional-Related Organizations

If you are in a job or a profession where there are organizations set up to focus on your particular job or profession, joining such an organization might help you to set a goal to become an expert in your job or profession. Here are some examples, as described on the internet:

The Fresno Idea Works:

Causes: Arts and Culture, Arts Education, Computer Science, Education, Engineering and Technology, Technology

Mission: Our goal is to nurture ideas and provide assistance in equipment, knowledge, and skill sets to help incubate ideas, both fanciful and practical, as learning projects and as business incubators. We provide infrastructure and collaboration opportunities for people interested in programming, hardware hacking, physics, chemistry, mathematics, photography, security, robotics, all kinds of art, and, of course, technology.

ISACA

ISACA is a global association that provides IT professionals with knowledge, credentials, training and community in IS/IT audit, assurance, security, privacy, risk and governance.

The ISACA community—members, <u>volunteers</u> and professional staff—is guided by our Purpose and Promise, which define the essence of who we are and what we do. Our Purpose is the reason we exist—to help business technology professionals and their enterprises around the world realize the positive potential of technology. Our Promise is how we, as an organization and as individuals, deliver on our Purpose—the work we do every day to inspire confidence that enables innovation through technology. Our work, and the work of the more than 460,000 engaged business technology professionals we support, has never been more important.

AICPA

The American Institute of Certified Public Accountants is the national professional organization of Certified Public Accountants in the United States, with more than 418,000 members in 143 countries in business and industry, public practice, government, education, student affiliates and international associates. Wikipedia

What does it mean to be an AICPA member?

It means you are connected to a professional network 400,000 strong. It means you receive support and guidance for the work you do every day. And it means you are challenged to seize that next career milestone.

TIA

The Telecommunications Industry Association (TIA) represents the entire supply chain of companies that build and support the communications technologies and information networks of today and tomorrow. The TIA website explains:

"For more than 90 years we have earned the trust of the world's most recognized Information and Communications Technology (ICT) brands that serve the global marketplace across every industry. While our name has changed, our mission to accelerate connectivity, encourage investment and drive innovation, jobs and economic opportunity hasn't."

****

Becoming a member of a professional organization provides numerous benefits, including boosting credibility and opportunities to cultivate contacts in the industry.

PERSONAL BENEFITS OF VOLUNTEERING

Some of the possible benefits of becoming a member of an organization and becoming a volunteer for the organization are personal education, serving on committees, speaking at conferences, instructing others, writing articles, serving in leadership positions at the organization, and becoming a recognized expert in your field.

Personal Education

Many of the job-related or professional-related organizations provide training programs for its members on topics that will help you gain more knowledge for your specific skill needs. In addition, some of these organizations have training programs that result, if you pass the examinations, in awarding you a certificate, acknowledging that you have achieved a specialized skill level. For example, ISACA, mentioned earlier, has certificate programs for Certified Information System Auditors (CISA), for Certified Information Security Managers (CISM), and for other skills. Such certificates are valuable to show employers or prospective employers that you have skills they need or will need in the future.

Serving on Committees

Generally, these organizations have a committee structure that brings together members to study the needs of its members and to provide guidance, develop training programs, develop new ideas or concepts, develop new methodologies, and create standards of acceptable behavior for its members.

As a member of the organization, you can be on the receiving end of such development issues, or you can be on the forefront of the development of the issues (by volunteering for committee assignments), or you can do both.

The positioning of your involvement depends on your desire to become a leader in the organization, the effort you want to put into the development side of the organization, your skill level at the time, your enthusiasm for the subjects being considered for development, and time you have available. Making TIME to become involved with the activities of the organization as a volunteer, taking into consideration the work/life balance discussed earlier, can provide you with experiences that might be invaluable for your future success in business and in life.

LIFE HACKS

Instructing Others

Training others in your own company or in any industrial or professional organization is an excellent way to start learning about public speaking. Unless, of course, you were part of a debate team in high school or college.

Once you obtain a level of knowledge that can be passed on to other employees or organization members, becoming a part of a training team is an excellent start to becoming a public speaker.

Speaking at Conferences

How and why might you be asked to speak at an industry and professional conference?

If your committee has developed a new training program for the members, has created a new methodology, has developed a new business model, or is issuing new standards for its members, then the committee has something to communicate. One way to communicate these matters to its members is presenting the matters to the members via conferences.

If you have been intimately involved in the process and if you are or have experience as a speaker or presenter, you might be asked to communicate the results of the committee work or research at such a conference. Should you take on such an assignment? I would suggest that you should agree to be a speaker, if you have taken a public speaking course or class or if you feel comfortable speaking before a large group of fellow members.

Speaking at conferences can improve your own self-confidence, your public speaking confidence, and can showcase your knowledge to these audiences. Such appearances can lead to other speaking requests from your organization or from other organizations

65

who want you to speak to their members. These speaking engagements can start you on the road to becoming a leading knowledge sharer and potentially a leader in your organization or in your profession.

Writing Articles

Why should you consider writing articles, books or internet blogs? Simply, it is a way, for example, to share views, ideas, **data, information, knowledge, wisdom**, specific skills, and historical events. Writing articles can give you an opportunity to share your knowledge with other workers and fellow professionals and can give you the platform to present yourself as an expert in your field.

Why did I highlight the four matters in the preceding paragraph? Because it is a known concept that to create **wisdom**, you need the steps of organizing **data**, from which you create **information**, from which you create **knowledge**, and from which leads you to **wisdom**.

Writing articles can help you pass on your wisdom to the world.

Leadership

Can anyone be a leader? Generally, not! Otherwise, there would be chaos in the world.

It is a long-held historical belief that Christopher Columbus discovered the Americas. Was Columbus a leader? Absolutely. Could any other person be a leader like Columbus? Yes, we have many, many instances of leaders like him: Ferdinand Magellan, Vasco da Gama, Amerigo Vespucci, presidents of countries, presidents of companies, and on and on. All are leaders in their respective fields.

According to "Inc.com,"

>"The best leaders are those who seek every opportunity to communicate and mentor others in an effort to clarify team objectives."

Warren Bennis of the University of Southern California defines leadership somewhat as:

>"The capacity to translate vision into reality, in that leadership defines what the future should look like, aligns people with that vision, and inspires them to make it happen, despite the obstacles."

Would you consider yourself a leader or do you think you could become a leader?

If you have the desire to lead and have the leadership skills to lead, then you might become a leader. Perhaps in your job or profession you have not yet had the opportunity to show your leadership skills. However, by volunteering in an industrial or in a professional organization, you may be presented with a leadership opportunity.

Many of these organizations are non-profits, and many of the leadership positions are filled by volunteer members. If you work in various volunteer positions and work with the present leaders, you may be recognized for your efforts, knowledge, skills, and, yes, leadership skills. Thus, giving you an opportunity to be a leader before you, possibly, become a leader in your company or your profession.

Recognized Expert

How does a person become a recognized expert? Possibly, by doing all the above.

Personal Example

I have been a volunteer all my life. Possibly, I learned from my father who was a volunteer fireman during the depression years. As I mentioned, I started by volunteering as an altar boy, I became the captain of my CYO basketball team, joined the NY State Society of CPA Candidates, the NY State Society Auditing Standards and Procedures Committee, became the Chairman of the AICPA's EDP Auditing Standards Subcommittee of the Auditing Standards Board, became a member of the AICPA's Auditing Standards Board, member of ISACA's Standards Board, member of the International Federation of Accountants (IFAC) EDP Auditing Standards Subcommittee, Chairman of the Board of Directors of ISACA, Chairman of IFAC's International Auditing and Assurance Standards Board (formally, named the International Auditing Practices Committee), member of IFAC's Consultative Advisory Committee to its International Auditing and Assurance Standards Board, as well as many, many other volunteer organizations.

Because of such volunteer positions, I was able to travel the world, made presentations all over the world, wrote articles, made life-long friends, had incredible FUN, met heads of state, consulted with numerous international organizations, spoke at the European Union with simultaneous translations into eight languages, and became a recognized leader in my volunteer organizations and in my profession.

How did all of this happen? I believe I can trace it back to my senior year in college. My auditing professor brought a new auditing standard into class one day. He passed the printed standard to us and on the back was a listing of the committee members who developed the standard. I asked the professor who these people were.

He said that they were members of the profession who had developed an expert level of knowledge about auditing and were asked to join the Committee to develop standards for the auditing profession.

At that point, I said to myself that I wanted to be involved in that aspect of the profession and not to be just a worker in the profession. I tried to stay true to that concept throughout my accounting career.

CHAPTER 13

MAKING SOMETHING HAPPEN – TAKING RISKS – DO NOT FEAR FAILURE

Principle: *"Do not wait for something to affect your life—make it happen yourself."*

Many financial and business gurus talk about looking beyond your environment, to look to the future, to look to innovation and to make something happen in your life and in your business.

These gurus also talk about how you will not be able to succeed without taking risks.

They also talk about not fearing failure.

Make Something Happen

If you get on a bicycle but you do not peddle, you will not go anywhere. In order to make something happen with the bicycle, you **must** peddle.

It is like anything in life. If you want to get married, you **must** ask the other person. If you want to get a job, you **must** apply for a position. Therefore, using the word "must" in your life becomes a new imperative in your life.

In the business world, in order to make something happen, in simple terms, you need to consider if change is necessary. If you are a product manager, do you keep making the same product year after year, or do you see how you can make the product better/more useful? Do you look to see if the product needs to be redesigned or reengineered? Or do you see if something entirely new can replace the existing product? These are all things a good product manager **must** consider. These are all things that a good product manager does to "make something happen."

In the above example, if the product manager does not try to innovate and does not try to make something happen, then someone else or a competitor might and there is a risk that your product will become obsolete.

The point of this section is if you do not innovate, change, and make something happen, then you and, perhaps, your company might stagnate. To me, the concepts of innovation and change can make our jobs more interesting, challenging and, yes, more fun.

Taking Risks

Should we be taking risks in life and in business? Again, absolutely! If we do not take risks, then we lose the opportunity to move forward.

Take a skier, for example. In order to ski at most ski areas, a skier must sign a waiver of indemnity to ski, absolving the ski operator of liability. Do we still ski? Of course, we do. If we did not sign the waiver, we would not be able to ski. So, we take the risk of signing and we go out and ski. Is skiing a risky sport? Yes, it is. But what do we do? We, to an extent, mitigate those risks by taking ski lessons, by being careful in our skiing, by observing the rules of skiing, and by watching out for other skiers who do not observe such rules. So, we take risks, but we can, sometimes, mitigate those risks.

In business, it can be the same. We take risks on new ventures and we set up processes and procedures to try mitigating risks of failure. Nonetheless, failures can occur because other businesses have a better product or service or because circumstances beyond our control causes failure, such as the pandemic of 2020.

Fearing Failure

Again, the gurus discuss how we should not be afraid of failure. Fear of failure can be when that fear stops us doing what is needed to achieve our goals. The gurus have also told us that many people have failed, but it did not stop them from learning from their experiences and moving on to a successful new business opportunity.

Therefore, in my mind, fear of failure should be recognized, but we should keep it way back in the recesses of our mind, and it should not stop us from taking risks and making something happen.

Personal Example

How did I make things **happen** in my life and in my business career? Here are some examples:

- When I started working in my accounting firm, I went to our personal department (now called Human Resources) and said, since I was single, I would be pleased to take out-of-town assignments.

- When I read about my firm having IBM training on programming punch card machines, I asked to be involved and was sent to a five-week training program at IBM. This training set me on my course of getting into computer technology and control over such technology.
- I asked to be considered for an overseas assignment.
- I went to Japan twenty days after getting married.
- Upon returning from Japan, I started employing computer auditing techniques on my audit assignments.
- The audit division head in the New York office heard about my work and asked me to accompany him to our World Headquarters to make a presentation to our Board of Partners.
- I was then asked to Chair a committee of partners from around the world to further develop my concepts.
- We ultimately developed a new audit methodology that was implemented worldwide.
- I led the development of the firm's computer audit software for mainframe systems.
- I set up the first microcomputer task force with partners representing audit, tax, small business, and consulting.
- I arranged to meet at Microsoft with Bill Gates to work on the beta version of Excel, discuss the future of microcomputer software, and arranged to license the Microsoft suite of software for worldwide use in my firm.
- I proposed the development of a new group to focus on computer audit specialists to assist our audit teams in auditing clients with complex computer systems, and to use such specialists to also perform consulting work in off-seasons. I started with three staff.

- Ultimately, the group grew worldwide to over five hundred specialists with revenues of over five hundred million dollars per year.

Were there **risks** involved with any of the above matters? Absolutely. But if you do not try to take risks, then you will not try to make things happen. For example, if I did not try to take risks in moving to auditing in a computer environment, then my firm, perhaps, might have been late in recognizing the environmental changes relating to use of computers and the need to control the date flow through those computers occurring at our clients.

Was there a fear of **failure** involved with any of the above matters? Yes, of course. For example, in transferring to Japan, would my wife and I be able to adopt to a society different from our own? Would I be able to work in an accounting system completely unlike the accounting system in the United States? Would my wife be happy in Japan? Would we be able to learn Japanese?

To mitigate and offset some of these fears, before going to Japan, we studied the culture of Japan, read books, and prepared ourselves for this change in the most **positive** manner possible.

CHAPTER 14

UNDERSTANDING THE BUSINESS – GOVERNANCE AND STRATEGY

Principle: *"Organizational knowledge helps leaders succeed."*

In chapter eight, I discussed getting to know your company, its business, and its industry, all as part of starting to increase your knowledge, to increase your skill level, and to focus on becoming an expert in your job or profession. This chapter is designed to focus your attention on the entity employing you and to get a better understanding of its business so you can focus on the next stage of your development and how you can help your entity/company develop and grow.

For you to be part of this development and growth, there are a number of concepts for you to understand such as the Governance of an entity, its Mission Statement, its Code of Conduct, its Strategic Plan, its Business Plan, and its Risk Management and Risk Profile.

Governance

What is Governance? Basically, it involves a broad category of management matters under an overall term of Governance. In getting to know about your enterprise, I have put this topic first because of its extreme importance. Unless an entity has a good governance structure, it might be very difficult to operate the entity's business or services in an organized and controlled structural environment. If your organization does not have a good governance structure, it might not provide you with an opportunity experience to succeed. On the other hand, it might provide you with an opportunity to help institute such a structure.

Thus, Governance can include such matters as Corporate Governance, Enterprise Governance, Enterprise Governance and the Extended Enterprise, and IT Governance. A brief summary of these matters are as follows:

Corporate Governance

According to "encycogov.com, Mathiesen [2002]":

"Corporate governance is a field in economics that investigates how to secure/motivate efficient management of corporations by the use of incentive mechanisms, such as contracts, organizational designs and legislation. This is often limited to the question of improving financial performance, for example, how the corporate owners can secure/motivate that the corporate managers will deliver a competitive rate of return."

According to "A Case for Global Corporate Governance Rules: An Auditor's Perspective." Robert S. Roussey, International Journal of Auditing, 2000, Corporate Governance is:

"The ethical corporate behavior by directors or others charged with governance in the creation and preservation of wealth for all stakeholders."

Enterprise Governance

According to the Board Briefing on IT Governance, Second Edition, IT Governance Institute, 2003:"

"Enterprise governance is a set of responsibilities and practices exercised by the board and executive management with the goal of providing strategic direction, ensuring that objectives are achieved, ascertaining that risks are managed appropriately and verifying that the enterprise's resources are used responsibly."

Enterprise Governance and the Extended Enterprise

According to "Governance of the Extended Enterprise: Bridging Business and IT Strategies, the IT Governance Institute, John Wiley & Sons, 2005":

The Extended Enterprise* operates outside its traditional boundaries:

• From areas of sales-force automation, customer service, technical support, workgroup collaboration, forms processing, order entry, knowledge management systems, and information delivery within and without the enterprise.
• To collaboration with other enterprises on the design, development, engineering, production, and delivery of new products, systems, or services, where both enterprises contribute their specific knowledge and skills.

IT Governance

According to "Robert S. Roussey, Board Briefing on IT Governance, Second Edition, IT Governance Institute, 2003":

> "IT governance is the term used to describe how those persons entrusted with governance of an entity will consider IT in their supervision, monitoring, control and direction of the entity. How IT is applied within the entity will have an immense impact on whether the entity will attain its vision, mission or strategic goals."

The entire topic of Governance is extremely interesting and is critical for good management and control of business and government entities. The above discussion of Governance aspects is only a slight glimpse of the topic and is one that should be studied as part of developing a well-rounded skill set.

Mission Statement

The Mission Statement of a business or other entity is simply "what do we want to do."

According to Investopedia:

> "A mission statement is used by a company to explain, in simple and concise terms, its purpose(s) for being."

A more descriptive definition might be

> "A Mission Statement is a formal summary of the aims, goals and values of a company or organization, and is a statement to which all employees can understand and subscribe"

For example, the Mission Statement of the Walt Disney Company is:

"The **mission** of The **Walt Disney Company** is to entertain, inform and inspire people around the globe through the power of unparalleled storytelling, reflecting the iconic brands, creative minds and innovative technologies that make ours the world's premier entertainment company."

Thus, the Walt Disney Company wants its employees to be part of its unparalleled storytelling to continue in its mission to be the world's premier entertainment company. An employee who finds storytelling fascinating would do well in helping the Company achieve this mission as compared to an employee who does not understand the employee's role in achieving the mission of the company.

Sometimes, an organization might have a Mission Statement that also morphs into a Vision Statement (i.e., a statement that reflects the entity's vision on how the entity wants to affect a community or the world).

For example, the World Bank's Mission Statement is

"To end extreme poverty: By reducing the share of the global population that lives in extreme poverty to 3 percent by 2030. To promote shared prosperity: By increasing the incomes of the poorest 40 percent of people in every country."

The World Bank's Vision Statement is

"The World Bank Group is one of the world's largest sources of funding and knowledge for developing countries. Its five institutions share a commitment to reducing poverty, increasing shared prosperity, and promoting sustainable development."

Thus, if you want to become an employee of the World Bank, you should have a set of altruistic values and a desire to help eradicate poverty around the world. If you do, you will stand a better chance of success then an employee who just wants a job.

Code of Conduct

According to "ethics.com":

> "A well-written **code of conduct** clarifies an organization's mission, values and principles, linking them with standards of professional conduct."

Why did I use a quote from "ethics.com?" In my mind, it is all about **ethics in business and in government**. If our leaders in business and in government establish Codes of Conduct for its employees to work in an **"ethical environment,"** then we reduce the chances for fraud, corruption, mismanagement, anarchy, and unaccountability. However, for these codes to be effective, the leaders at the top (Tone at the Top) should emphatically promote them to the organization, indicating that there will be no tolerance about lack of adhering to such policies. In addition, there should be procedures established to make sure the policies are being followed.

Codes of Conduct and Codes of Ethics are often combined into one document for ease of establishing such policies and for employees to use.

According to "Betterteam.com":

> "A code of ethics and professional conduct outlines the ethical principles that govern decisions and behavior at a company or organization. They give general outlines of how employees should behave, as

well as specific guidance for handling issues like harassment, safety, and conflicts of interest."

An entity's Code of Conduct, in my mind, is one of the most important set of principles established in business and government entities. I suggest that it should be one of the principles that you study and follow in your career.

Strategic Plan

According to The Balanced Scorecard Institute:

"A **strategic plan** is a document used to communicate with the organization the organizations goals, the actions needed to achieve those goals and all of the other critical elements developed during the **planning** exercise."

The Balanced Scorecard Institute has created tools and methodologies for entities to use in establishing a Strategic Plan. For example, shown below, from the Balanced Scorecard Institute's website, is something termed a strategy map.

The Institute describes the strategy map as "a simple graphic that shows a logical, cause-and-effect connection between strategic objectives (shown as ovals on the map). It is one of the most powerful elements associated with the balanced scorecard methodology, as it is used to quickly communicate how value is created by the organization. Strategy mapping can vastly improve any strategy communication effort. Most people are visual learners and so a picture of your strategy will be understood by many more employees than a written narrative. Plus, the process of developing a strategy map forces the team to agree on what they are trying to accomplish in simple, easy-to-understand terms. With a well-designed strategy map, every employee can see how they contribute to the achievement of the organization's objectives."

An illustration of the strategy map follows:

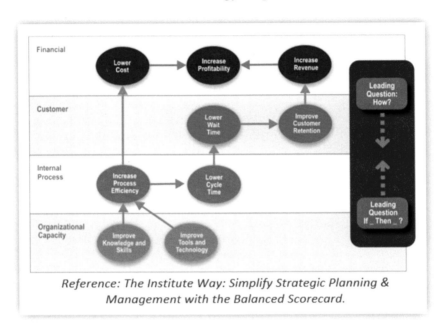

Reference: The Institute Way: Simplify Strategic Planning & Management with the Balanced Scorecard.

If you are working for an entity that has a Strategic Plan, and it is available to all employees, then I would suggest that you get it, read, and study it, and see how you fit into the overall plan as you plan your own strategies for success within the organization. If you are working for an entity that does not have a Strategic Plan, then I would suggest that you study Strategic Planning Methodology, then find a way to present this planning methodology to the management of your company, working within, if necessary, the organization's chain of command.

If someone above you in the chain of command steals your idea and ultimately take credit for it, then it illustrates the Code of Conduct is not working or that individual is not adhering to it.

Business Plan

The concepts of Governance, Mission Statements, and Strategic Plans are only part of the picture of knowing or building a business. Can you start or develop a business entity without having a business plan? Yes, you can. But should you do so without developing such a plan. Probably, not!

According to Nationwide (the insurance company):

"Whether you are starting a small **business** or exploring ways to expand an existing one, a **business plan** is an **important** tool to help guide your decisions. Think of it as a roadmap to success, providing greater clarity on all aspects of your business, from marketing and finance to operations and product/service details."

According to "Entrepurenur.com," there are fifteen reasons why you need a Business Plan:

1) Grow your existing business.

2) Back up a business loan application.

3) Seek investment for a business, whether it is a startup or not.

4) Create a new business.

5) Valuation of the business for formal transactions related to divorce, inheritance, estate planning, and tax issues.

6) Sell your business.

7) Deal with professionals.

8) **Develop new business alliances.**

9) **Share and explain business objectives with your management team, employees, and new hires.**

10) Decide whether you need new assets, how many, and whether to buy or lease them.

11) Hire new people.

12) Decide whether to rent new space.

13) Deal with displacement.

14) Share your strategy, priorities, and specific action points with your spouse, partner or significant other.

15) Set specific objectives for managers.

All the above are good reasons for business planning. For purposes of this chapter, I would like to focus on the reasons highlighted in black above.

In getting to know the business, you need to need to understand (1) management's business objectives, (2) the specific objectives management has set for its managers, and (3) management's development of new business alliances.

If you can obtain a good understanding of these business objectives and development plans, you can, again, see how you fit into the business and see how you can become part of the business development alliances. In our current and future business environment, we are starting to see more and more alliances with other entities in the same industry and with alliances with entities in other industries. For example, **Pfizer** is part of a robust cancer **alliance** that includes the cancer research collaborations and **partnerships** to develop breakthroughs in cancer treatment.

The same would be appropriate in a government or civic environment. If the government officials clearly set forth their objectives for each of their departments, set forth their objectives for the managers of the departments, and set forth their alliances with other governmental/civic entities, you as an employee can see how you can play your part in achieving those objectives. In governments, a good example of alliances is the North Atlantic Treaty Organization (NATO).

Risk Management and Risk Profile

What is a Risk Profile? Basically, it is a process to **identify and manage** internal and external risks to an entity. Is it easy to develop a Risk Profile for a business or governmental agency? For a small business or a single governmental agency in a local municipality, it should not be too difficult or take a great deal of time. In a large business or in a large city government, it could be very time consuming and complex.

Some illustrative steps, on establishing a Risk Profile for Risk Management in an enterprise (business, non-profit, or government), for each aspect of the enterprise's activities, are

- Collecting data to enable effective risk identification.
- Analyze these risks in order to develop useful information supporting risk decisions that consider the relevance of risk factors, such as internal and external treats and vulnerabilities.
- Maintain a risk profile comprising an inventory of these identified risks, including (1) expected frequency of occurrence, (2) potential impact on the entity, and (3) the controls established to minimize occurrence and impact on the entity.
- Articulate the risks to the management responsible for the assets or processes impacted by the applicable risks.
- Manage risks by seizing opportunities to reduce risks to an acceptable level.
- React to events by seizing opportunities to limit the size of loss.
- Establish and maintain a common risk view by aligning the risks with the enterprise risk objectives.

- Make risk-aware business decisions that consider the full range of opportunities and consequences of these decisions.
- Integrate the individual activities of the entity with the overall Enterprise Risk Management Profile.

The above discussion only provides a brief indication of the time and effort required to establish a Risk Profile in a medium to large enterprise.

Take, for example, a credit card enterprise. The enterprise knows, intuitively, that there will be credit card losses to be absorbed by it. One of the key issues faced by the enterprise is how to mitigate those potential losses. Thus, systems are established to track credit card transactions, to determine spending profiles of its customers, to identify unusual transactions going into a customer's account, to identify fraudulent transactions, to issue new cards relating to lost or stolen customer cards, to enable customers to lock and unlock a card if the customer thinks it is lost or stolen, and on and on.

Thus, the Risk Profile is another strategic aspect of management's focus on business development and its control over the development process.

As an employee/manager of an enterprise, Risk Management and Risk Profiles are part of enterprise management and is a topic you should study and consider in your overall skill development process.

Personal Example

Governance. I became involved with the topic of governance through my audit work in considering the business of my clients, how management controlled or did not control their organizations, and through my involvement with ISACA. Because of my interest and the importance of this topic, I made numerous presentations on the subject around the world and wrote several articles on it.

Mission Statements. I remember the mission of the firm I joined many years ago was something like:

1. Hire the best people.
2. Provide the best training possible to them.
3. Empower them to provide outstanding services to our clients.

These basic concepts were the key driving forces to achieve success as a firm, and the concepts stayed with me during my entire career. However, as our firm's clients continued to expand to locations around the world, our mission had to focus, additionally, on the expansion of the firm to offices in other countries (growth), to continue our focus on the ethical aspects of our work, and to focus on a one-firm concept.

Code of Conduct. One of the first fraud instances I encountered was the salad oil scandal of 1963. On the day John F. Kennedy, the President of the United States, was assassinated, I was on the top of a massive holding tank owned by Allied Crude Vegetable Oil Company. I was auditing the loan trust receipts for four million barrels of salad oil on the books of a client. I was doing a test of the salad oil to verify the loan trust receipts. What we found was a holding talk of #6 crude oil and not salad oil. The rest was history. Anthony De Angelis, a commodities trader, and Allied's founder, eventually served seven years in prison for fraud and conspiracy.

This scandal ultimately caused over $180 million ($1.5 billion today) in losses to companies involved, including my client.

Strategic Plan. During my term as International President of ISACA and on its Board of Directors, we focused on Strategic Planning and on the Balanced Scorecard Institute's methodology promulgated by the Institute. This was a very valuable learning experience as ISACA continued its growth as a professional organization.

Business Plan. My son and his business partner asked me to provide funding for their proposed virtual business (i.e., a business that would virtually run without much of their involvement). My first requirement was to have them develop a business plan. Their plan was excellent, and I funded their enterprise. In my own firm, I had to develop a business plan for my partners to approve in setting up the computer audit specialist teams mentioned earlier.

Risk Management and Risk Profile. One of the great things about volunteering is becoming involved in various technologies. My involvement with ISACA's Board allowed me to be part of developing a Risk Profile for ISACA, together with an outside consulting firm.

CHAPTER 15

UNDERSTANDING THE ORGANIZATIONAL INPUTS TO YOUR BUSINESS AND APPLYING YOUR SKILL SETS TO THE ORGANIZATIONAL INPUTS

Principle: *"Understanding, knowledge and creativity can help you shape the future."*

In this chapter, I will endeavor to describe various inputs and I will focus on business organizations. What do I mean by "inputs" to a business? I am using the term "inputs" to mean the various external factors that can affect the business and how management needs to react to those inputs. While some of the inputs may be easy to spot, consider, and react, others may not be so obvious. Some of these inputs are

- Capital needs and deployment
- Changing business processes
- Innovation by Other businesses
- Hiring employees

- Input Forces requiring innovation within the business
- Government regulations
- Customer needs

Capital Needs and Deployment

Management of a business must strike a balance between using capital for operating expenses verses using capital for investment in buildings, equipment, acquisitions, and research and development. The outside inputs can relate to obsolete equipment due to competitive forces, new technology, and customer requests. For example, the *New York Times* and the *Wall Street Journal* had to expand and invest in new online news technology with subscription services to compete with other news sources on the internet.

Changing Business Processes

As we move into a Fourth Industrial Revolution, we need to consider how to change business processes to compete in this changing environment. For example, Amazon's online shopping has changed the customer focus from stores to the internet, causing disruption to investments (leases) in shopping malls, as well as significant disruption to the owners of the shopping malls. Management of consumer businesses around the world has reacted by establishing internet web sites for marketing and sales of their products. Owners of shopping malls must reimagine and reengineer their malls to make them relevant in today's environment.

Innovation by Other Businesses

If other competing companies are moving to new technologies, do you have the capital and employee skills to do likewise? For example, are you the "horse and buggy" company or are you the "automobile" company?

Do you need to plan ahead? For example, Teledyne Technologies indicates "Teledyne provides enabling technologies for industrial growth markets. We have evolved from a company that was primarily focused on aerospace and defense to one that serves multiple markets that require advanced technology and high reliability. These markets include deep water oil and gas exploration and production, oceanographic research, air and water quality environmental monitoring, factory automation and medical imaging."

Hiring Employees

One of the most important matters for employers to consider is hiring employees in consideration of outside inputs affecting their businesses. As business practices evolve, as we move into the Fourth Industrial Revolution, the hiring practices for the employee of the future evolves. As Teledyne evolves, the need for employees skilled in applicable fields to implement their new technologies also evolves.

Input Forces Requiring Innovation Within the Business

Forward looking management will recognize the changing environment and will start changing its business from within the business. For example, Pfizer recognized that products coming out of the patent protection stage will go into the generic product category. Thus, Pfizer entered a new venture with Mylan that will put all its generic drugs into the new venture, leaving Pfizer to focus on new drug research and development and sales.

Government Regulations

The inputs from government regulations in the United States and applicable regulations in other countries have or may have a direct effect on the business practices of a company. Changes in tax, anti-trust, securities, employment, discrimination, environmental, and similar laws and regulations need to be studied and evaluated for impacts on the business.

Customer Needs

In past years, companies made products or developed services based on what management believed the customer needed. In today's environment, the customer focus has changed considerably. Companies now meet extensively with their customers to elicit input from them on their wants and desires. These inputs are taken into consideration in determining what changes are need to products or services and what new products or services need to be developed.

Personal Example

As mentioned earlier, because of changing environmental inputs from our clients, e.g., computerization and resulting process flow changes, it was imperative that changes had to be made in our auditing process. As we developed the new audit process, we included a methodology to evaluate the appropriateness of our clients' internal controls. This methodology was finished when the Foreign Corrupt Practices Act of 1977 was passed by Congress. The accounting provisions of the Act required companies to devise and maintain systems of internal control to meet various requirements. Our new audit methodology was ahead of the legislation.

Early in the formation of ISACA, inputs from our members

focused on internal control as a key aspect of information technology. As a result, volunteer members, over the years, developed "Control Objectives for Information Technology" (COBIT) that eventually became a much broader methodology, available to its members and to entities around the world, for overall management and control of information technology environments.

CHAPTER 16

SAVING FOR RETIREMENT

Principle: *"The earlier you can start saving for retirement, the better chance you will have in creating a comfortable retirement."*

In my view, saving for retirement starts with your first savings account, as long as that account is opened when you are about six years old. In reality, for many, it is when you are first employed. Saving even a few dollars for retirement is a good start. As you start to accumulate some "free" cash, putting a larger amount out of your pay is an even better start. Why? Because of the so-called "magic of compound interest."

According to the *New York Times*:

"You've probably read about this before, but the best way to understand it is to see it in front of you.

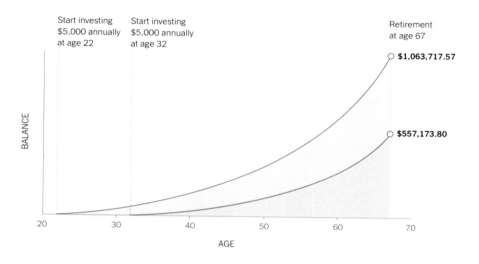

Yes, we did that math correctly. If two people put the same amount of money away each year ($5,000), earn the same return on their investments (6 percent annually), and stop saving upon retirement at the same age (67), one will end up with nearly twice as much money just by starting at twenty-two instead of thirty-two. Put another way: The investor who started saving ten years earlier would have about five hundred thousand dollars more at retirement. It's that simple."

Is it really that simple? Yes, it is if you can afford to start investing five thousand dollars annually. But most young people may not have that amount of money to save each year or may not have the inclination to do so.

As I mentioned in chapter one, the earlier you start thinking about your future, the earlier you can create your future. The same is true for saving for retirement: the earlier you can start saving for retirement, the better chance you will have in creating a comfortable retirement.

Retirement planning has been changing over the past several decades or so. Some of the original retirement plans were based on company or government plans that set up retirement accounts for its employees and, in effect, guaranteed a certain amount of money each month upon retirement. With certain tax law changes, we have started to see a change from these company-funded retirement plans to individual savings plans.

Some of these individual savings plans have tax deferred features, various limitations, and other requirements, not discussed here, and include plans, such as

1. Individual Retirement Accounts (IRAs), for the self-employed or employees whose employers do not offer retirement plans. These plans are often set up by the individual at a bank or securities firm.

2. The termed 401-K plans established by for-profit organizations, for employees to establish savings accounts. Some of these organizations will have matching programs where the employer will match some of your savings, with certain limitations established by the employer. An employer may match up to 3 percent, 6 percent or higher amounts of your salary. This matching of your savings provides an even greater incentive to save as your retirement fund grows at a much faster rate.

3. The Keogh plan is designed for self-employed persons and their employees. A Keogh plan is similar to a 401-K plan but has higher annual contribution limits than the 401-K plans.

The above discussion is only meant to provide you with some indications as to how you might include IRAs and employer-based plans in your savings for retirement planning.

Personal Example

In thinking back, I did not think too much about retirement, but as mentioned earlier, I did think about savings and investing. When I became a partner in my firm is when I started to focus on retirement planning. The firm had a Keogh plan for its partners and I always put the maximum contribution into the plan. This was not too difficult because of my long-standing focus on savings and investing.

CHAPTER 17

LOOKING TO THE FUTURE AND MAKING CHANGES TO YOUR ORGANIZATION TO SURVIVE/DEVELOP THE FUTURE

Principle: *"Look to the Future."*

I have encouraged you to look to the future several times in this book. One thing I have not mentioned extensively is about looking to the future in the eyes of an entrepreneur and how this view can help your organization survive and develop in the Fourth Industrial Revolution.

Wikipedia describes an entrepreneur, in effect, as a person who creates a business and entrepreneurship as the process of designing, launching, and running a new business, which is often initially a small business.

Generally, an entrepreneur creates a business to bring an idea, a process, a concept, or a product to market, taking on greater than normal financial risks. Such a person looks to the future to determine if success is possible. The entrepreneur will do many of the matters previously discussed, such as developing a business plan, in developing the future of the business.

Can a person be an entrepreneur within an existing business? Yes. Let me explain.

Entrepreneurship, in a way, is like leadership, i.e., the leading of a group of people. If you are an entrepreneur starting a business, you are the leader of that business organization. If you are a leader in an organization, you can also be an entrepreneur in your organization.

However, to be a leader and entrepreneur in your organization, you need to

1. Know and understand your organization
2. Know and understand your industry
3. Look to the Future
4. Create/develop the Future

I have already discussed the first two of the above suggestions in previous chapters, so I will concentrate on the latter two aspects of leadership/entrepreneurship.

Look to the Future

One of the concepts discussed extensively in this book is looking to the future in all aspects of our lives. At many points in your employment or running your own business, you will need to look to the future to determine:

1. Where is your entity's place in the business/industry?
2. Do we need to change the business or is there a need to innovate or to develop new businesses to survive or grow?
3. If so, what do we need to change, innovate or develop?

Create/Develop the Future

There are many steps in changing, innovating, or developing a new business. I will focus on a simple four-step process of researching, finding an idea, developing the idea, and implementing the idea. The discussion will be brief because to do otherwise would require extensive writing, discussion, and presentation, which is not the purpose of this book.

Research

In the budgets of most businesses, there is generally a budget for research and development. Without research, there may be no future.

Idea

Ideas can come from research, from research that has gone wrong but which created an idea not expected, from stumbling on an idea while looking for something else, from a friend or colleague who presents you with an idea, from customers, from employees, or from other sources.

Development

The development stage, in effect, is taking the idea and planning what is needed to create a new service, process, or product. This stage requires a development plan that looks at feasibility, cost, time and acceptance.

Implement

The implementation stage, in effect, is to take the "finished" service, process, or product and put it into operation. For example, for a new manufacturing process of a product, once the process is tested and accepted as a working process, the process is then implemented, and it starts the manufacturing of the new products.

Personal Example

In a previous chapter, I discussed my focus on the development of the new computer audit specialist program to help audit teams auditing complex computer environments. Here are two other examples of the concepts discussed in this chapter.

First example. Because I was on the editorial boards of a number of publications, I was asked to read and vet (i.e., peer review) articles submitted for publication. In reading one of these research articles, a research paper on a "moment bound" theory, I became intrigued on the possibility of using this concept as the basis for a new audit methodology tool. I called the research professor and discussed the potential for its use, but he could not see how it could be put into practical use. I called another research professor friend who agreed that it might work. Thus, we had Research and an Idea. The three of us started working on a Development of my idea using the moment bound theory, and after a three-year period, we completed this step, which included a computerized version of the methodology tool. Once the new tool was tested and accepted, it was Implemented on a world-wide basis in my firm.

Second example. One of the audit standards in the audit of financial statements is to consider whether the entity is a going concern at the time of the audit. In simple terms, an auditor had to consider whether the entity would continue to be a going concern for a certain period of time in the future from the date of the audit. This concept intrigued me as an auditor and businessman, and I wondered if financial distress/bankruptcy could be predicted with some degree of certainty. In researching this question, I found an article written by a finance professor on a bankruptcy predictive model he developed. Thus, my <u>Research</u> resulted in an <u>Idea</u> for a new predictive model for financial distress. I called the finance professor and he agreed to work with me on the <u>Development</u> of a new predictive model which would use multiple discriminate analysis. A basic model was developed for the manufacturing industry and the model was adopted for different industries, all with a resulting high degree of confidence in the predictability of financial distress/bankruptcy. The development included a microcomputer version for ease of use by our audit teams. Once the new tool was tested and accepted, it was <u>Implemented</u> on a world-wide basis in my firm. The tool was also licensed to others, including a major bank that used it as part of its due diligence in evaluating and approving loans. As a further example of innovation in business, in applying this predictive model to one of my clients with floating rate debt and significant investment in long-term assets, I was able to show that the company's financial stability was in the lowest 20 percentile of all publicly-traded companies in the United States. This analysis went to the management and board of directors of the company. Management immediately started to focus on its policies regarding investing in its long-term assets and how to move the floating rate debt to fixed rate debt. The management also asked me to apply the predictive model to all twenty-five competitors in the industry as a comparison to my client's own predictive score.

CHAPTER 18

WRITING AND SPEAKING TO OTHERS ABOUT THE CURRENT/ FUTURE CHANGES IN AND TO YOUR BUSINESS AND INDUSTRY

Principle: *"Sharing your knowledge and experience helps others and society."*

How do we share data, information, knowledge, and wisdom to others once we are out of the college or university environment? Basically, this sharing is done through in-company training, seminars, conventions, social media, blogs, professional or industry membership organizations, the setting of national and international professional standards, newspapers, articles, television, the internet, and other similar means.

On a Global level, we share this knowledge and experience through organizations such as:

- The Organization for Economic Co-operation and Development (OECD), mentioned earlier, is an international organization focused on building better policies for better lives.
- The World Bank, focusing on eliminating poverty and providing assistance to the poor.
- The International Monetary Fund, focusing on fostering global monetary cooperation.
- The United Nations, focusing on keeping world peace and improving living conditions for people around the world.

These organizations meet with its country members to research and share data, information, knowledge, and even, sometimes, wisdom among their members to promote cooperation in trying to achieve their goals.

On the national level, we share this knowledge and experience through similar business, professional, union, and government organizations that have been developed for similar purposes.

As an individual, can you participate in the information sharing? Again, yes, you can. I would encourage you to do so.

Remember my previous discussions on developing skills to become an expert in your field, on creating a work ethic, and on volunteering, all of which provide you with opportunities to accumulate data, information, knowledge and wisdom that you can share with others.

This sharing of your knowledge and wisdom is critical in building a better world and is critical for your own individual development.

Personal Example

In studying to take the Japanese CPA exam, I learned about the specific requirements and the role of the CPA in Japan. I decided to write an article, my first, on "The Certified Public Accountant in Japan," which was published in June 1968. I went on to write another thirty or so articles over the course of my career.

Another example is being part of professional committees where members from different firms and countries met to develop national and international standards. I was always amazed at how the members freely shared ideas, thoughts, and concepts to develop the best standards possible.

CHAPTER 19

PLANNING RETIREMENT

Principle: *"Waiting to plan retirement during retirement is not retirement."*

I started this book asking you to dream and focus on your future life. Now, we are at some point in the life process and I am asking you to think about retirement. When do you start "dreaming" about your retirement? I believe the time to dream or think about retirement is different for everyone.

One point I want to emphasize, at this time, is that your working life goes by in a flash. No sooner do you start working and the next moment, it seems, you are retired! In some sense, I am saying that building a career and a family makes the days and years go by so fast you hardly realize the passage of time.

When to Start Planning

So, again, the question is, when do you start planning for retirement? A good time might be for some at the time you receive your first paycheck. This gets back to the savings and investing discussion

106

because, in reality, it starts you off on the retirement road. Remember the chart in chapter sixteen that depicts retirement funds when someone starts saving at twenty-two or at thirty-two. The difference in the retirement results is quite substantial.

The planning described above is about the money flow, but it is not about actually planning for retirement. In the early part of your working life, you are more interested in your work and family than about your retirement. So, you may start to focus on retirement at some mid-point or more towards the later part of your working life. What are the retirement considerations when you do want to focus more on retirement? In my mind, the first focus item is a plan for retirement.

Plan for Retirement

One of the first matters to consider, when you do want to think seriously about retiring, is to develop a plan. The plan can be written or just thought about in your head. If you have a life partner, you need to sit down with your partner and start off the discussion as to what you both want to do in retirement. This is a critical first step because if you both cannot agree on a retirement plan, then it will be very difficult to create such a plan.

For example, what if your partner wants to buy an RV (recreational vehicle) and travel around the country and you want to settle in Florida and play golf? These are two opposite extremes, and you somehow have to find a common ground. Perhaps you meet a compromise that is agreeable to both of you, such as playing golf in Florida during the best months and traveling in an RV for the other months. Whatever is decided, there needs to be agreement at this point before starting to develop a more detailed plan.

At this point, you start the plan. Do you already have a home in Florida? Will you have to sell your existing home to have the money to purchase a home in Florida? Do you start researching areas in Florida that has good weather and accessible golf courses? Are home prices and golfing in these areas affordable? Do you need to visit these areas to see if they are as desirable as shows in the research literature? Do you start researching RVs? Do you rent an RV for a week and test out the RV experience? Getting both partners involved in retirement activities can get both interested and excited about retirement even many years before an actual retirement date.

As you plan, you will add more and more items to your plan. I will mention some of them below.

Health Considerations

Do you want to be healthy in retirement? Absolutely! Do you wait for retirement to think about your health? No! You need to consider your health all through your life. Some examples of good habits are

- Periodic physical examinations.
- Following physician instructions.
- Eating healthy food and maintaining a good diet.
- Maintaining a positive attitude.
- Social contacts with friends, family, and business associates.
- Not smoking and minimal indulgence with wine and alcohol.
- Exercise and maintaining an appropriate weight and body mass.

Thus, if you are following good health habits, you are actually planning for, hopefully, good health in your retirement years.

Wealth Creation

Upon actual retirement, do you want to (1) maintain a consistent lifestyle or (2) are you willing to accept a reduced lifestyle? If you want the first of the above two choices, then you want to focus on "wealth creation" as soon as possible. What does the term "wealth creation" mean?

Simply, it means the accumulation of assets, such as cash, investment securities, real estate, and bonds over a long period of time. In the concept of wealth creation for retirement, it should also include the accumulation of income producing assets. Income-producing assets during retirement are very important as the income (dividends or interest) offsets the use or spending of the retirement fund assets. A good example of wealth creation is having a retirement plan and retirement fund, such as the 401-K plan mentioned in a previous chapter.

Also, remember the discussions in chapter ten on Savings, particularly the section on Budgeting. In that section, there is a budgeting schedule estimating income and expenses for a year period, ending with the excess of income over expenses available for savings and investments. This budgeting process is an important part of planning for retirement.

Because in your budget planning you are also looking at how you can save and invest for retirement. Some of the maters to consider in budgeting and planning for wealth creation are:

- Do not try to keep up with or overshadow your friends or relatives in your purchases, i.e., do not try to "keep up with the Joneses."

- Live within your means.
- Purchase low-mileage previously owned cars.
- Purchase the smallest house in the best neighborhood.
- Purchase household items when you have the cash to do so.
- Pay off credit cards each month.
- Be frugal, but not miserly.

If your annual budget does not produce an excess for savings and investment, then you may need to reevaluate your budget for the year. An important point in this discussion is the interrelationships of what you need to do each year as you progress through life in relationship of your future retirement. In other words, what you do in your budgeting and planning is interrelated with wealth creation.

Is there a good way to track wealth creation? Yes, a good technique is to focus on "net worth." Net worth is your assets minus your liabilities. At the each of each year, list your assets and liabilities and calculate your net worth, and then list your net worth each year on a schedule of net worth by year. As intimated earlier, if your budget does not produce an excess for savings or investment, then you need to reevaluate your budget and change, if possible, your spending habits.

An illustration of an asset and liability schedule of net worth is as follows:

| ASSETS | 12/31/20x1 | December 31, 20x2 | | | |
		John R	John R Trust	Joint	Total
CASH					
Bank A - Checking Account	1	2			2
Bank A - Savings Account	1	2			2
Bank B - Checking Account	1			2	2
Bank B - Savings Account	1			2	2
	4	4	0	4	8
Bond Fund ABC	1	2			2
Securities					
Investment Banking Company A	1		3		3
Investment Banking Company B	1	2			2
	2	2	3	0	5
Real Estate					
Home A	500		600		600
Cabin B	50		60		60
	550	0	660	0	660
Automobiles					
Auto A	10	8			8
Auto B	10	8			8
	20	16	0	0	16
Retirement Funds and Insurance					
Vested Interest in 401-K	100	200			200
Personal IRA	20	25			25
Cash Value Life Insurance	30	35			35
	150	260	0	0	260
Total Assets	727	284	663	4	951
LIABILITIES					
Accounts Payable - Credit Cards	10	10			10
Mortgage on Home A	200	175			175
Income Taxes	10	15			15
Total Liabilities	220	200	0	0	200
NET WORTH	507	84	663	4	751

In the above example, John R. Jones' net worth at 12/31/20x1 is $507 and at 12/31/20x2 is $751. By listing each year's net worth on a separate schedule, it is easy to track the accumulation year by year.

Carryovers Into Retirement

What are these carryovers? Simply, they are the activities you have enjoyed all your life, such as swimming, jogging, tennis, exercising, sailing, surfing, reading, skiing, snowboarding, travel, teaching, volunteering, or helping others. In planning retirement, review these "carryovers" to determine those you would like to pursue. For example, if you want to continue tennis, then you might want to look for a golf club in Florida that also has a good tennis program. If you want to exercise, look for a club that has a good workout facility. I know people who joined a club with tennis facilities but did not have a good tennis program, thus requiring them to join another club.

The point of this carryover program is merely to remind you to consider, carefully, the type of activities you want to pursue in retirement and to be sure to include them in your planning.

Friendships

Hopefully, you have made friendships all your life, and they should become an important part of your retirement planning.

Who are the key friends and how do you want to be part of your retirement years? If you meet with and continually interact with these key friends, then they will become "carryovers" into your retirement years. If you only see some of the key friends infrequently, then they may not easily become carryovers. For this latter group of friends, you may want to start greater interactions with them in the five to ten years before your retirement.

Family

Making sure that your family relationships are in order and you are involved with their lives. Hopefully, you have good relationships with your family, and they will become an important part of your retirement.

Often, families drift apart during the working years or have disagreements. Perhaps in the years leading to retirement you can look to see how you can repair any such disagreeable relationships.

Assuming you have great family relationships, plan to have periodic days and meals with immediate family members and periodic family gatherings with the extended family. Annual gatherings of the extended family members are always times of fun and celebration.

Giving Back to Society

If you are able to, it is important to give back something of your success to society. This can mean volunteering at a community or retirement center, participating in community projects, establishing scholarship endowments at your college or university, or any one of a number of other ways to give back to society.

Personal Example

When to Start Planning

When I was forty-seven, my wife and I started planning retirement. The planning focused on a number of stages: (Stage One) retirement from my firm; (Stage Two) what we were going to do after the retirement, such as a new working, volunteer position for me; and (Stage Three) what we would do after Stage Two.

Plan for Retirement

Our plan for Stage One of retirement was to consider my firm's retirement program. The program included two facets: (1) mandatory retirement at age sixty-two or (2) early retirement starting at age fifty-five, under a program that provided a varying lump sum amount depending on the retirement year. One purpose of the early retirement program was to provide an opportunity for younger partners to enter the partnership at an earlier age. We agreed that I would retire at age fifty-five and decide what to after.

We did focus on where we would live in retirement. We decided, a place on a lake, a place on the ocean, a place in a ski resort, and a home on a golf course. Over the years, we did purchase a cabin on a lake, mentioned earlier; we did purchase an investment condo on the ocean; we did purchase a condo in a ski resort, so all we needed was a home in a golfing community.

Two years prior to my planned retirement at age fifty-five, I was asked to teach a course at one of the top graduate schools in the country. I did and found that I had a love for teaching at a university and, based on student evaluations, that I had the ability to be a great teacher. Thus entering into Stage Two of my retirement and becoming a professor, as mentioned previously. During this period, we sold our home in the North and built a home in a golfing community in Florida. Unfortunately, part way through Stage Two, upon completing the golfing community home, my wife died from an aneurism. I miss her! Stage Two and Stage Three had to be reassessed! I finally retired at age eighty, and I am now in Stage Three of retirement.

Health Considerations

Fortunately, all my life I tried to follow the guidance discussed above, including having a physical each year and following good health habits. For example, when the Surgeon General declared that smoking was not good for your health, I immediately stopped smoking. I have entered into Stage Three in a reasonably healthy manner.

Wealth Creation

Basically, I lived the guidance described in this book, including the preparation of the net worth schedule every year starting with the year I married.

Carryovers into Retirement

I have carried over many of the things we loved to do, including skiing, hiking, boating, reading, writing, exercising, traveling, and being with friends and family.

Friendships

Fortunately, many of the friends made over the years are still friends today. I have a new significant other, and our European friends visit us, and we visit them.

I collect French Bordeaux wines, and two of my colleagues from our ISACA days also collect wines. We are called the three Past Presents of ISACA, and every three months or so, we visit one of our respective "wine cellars" for a weekend of great food, conversations, camaraderie, and great wine.

Family

I have been fortunate to have had a loving and giving family relationship with my immediate and extended family.

Every year, we try to have a family reunion for as many family members as possible to attend.

Giving Back to Society

I have established several endowed scholarships at my university.

LAST THOUGHTS

Do not react negatively to the small things in life—they are not important—get along with family and friends—enjoy life—have fun—be kind—help one another—be positive—be ethical—and above all love those around you!

ROBERT S. ROUSSEY   **Appendix A**
Curriculum Vitae

Address   Mailing Address
Robert S. Roussey   Robert S. Roussey
Florida   E-mail: roussey@usc.edu

TEACHING BACKGROUND

UNIVERSITY OF SOUTHERN CALIFORNIA
        Professor of Clinical Accounting - September 1992 – August 2014, Retired

NORTHWESTERN UNIVERSITY, KELLOGG GRADUATE SCHOOL OF MANAGEMENT
        Adjunct Professor of Auditing   January–March 1990
                                             January–March 1991
        Faculty Honor Roll for Teaching   1990 Winter Quarter
        Faculty Honor Roll for Teaching   1991 Winter Quarter

ARTHUR ANDERSEN
        Instructor at numerous firm professional education courses and seminars, in the United States and countries around the world, on auditing, internal control, computer auditing, statistical sampling, accounting topics and related subjects, 1957 to 1992.

BUSINESS BACKGROUND

ARTHUR ANDERSEN

Partner and Director — Auditing Procedures, Chicago World Headquarters

Responsibilities — Developing firm policies in the areas of auditing in a computer environment, statistical sampling and other advanced audit techniques, and implementing a worldwide Computer Risk Management service line.

Member — Committee on Accounting Principles and Auditing Procedures - 1973–1977

Member — Management Advisory Committee on Information Systems - 1981–1985

Chairman or member of various other firm committees

Extensive experience as engagement partner on a number of the firm's largest multi-billion-dollar international clients, mainly in the industrial and natural resource areas, and in other industries, including government contracting, consumer, banking and brokerage fields. Extensive firmwide experience in developing auditing methodologies, practice tools and training programs, and in implementing these in the Firm's offices throughout the world.

1957–1965 - New York Office

1965–1969 - Tokyo Office

1969–1977 - New York Office

1977–1992 - Chicago World Headquarters

1992 - Retired

CPA in U.S.A. (New York State, retired) and in Japan

ACADEMIC BACKGROUND

FORDHAM UNIVERSITY, 1957 BACHELOR OF SCIENCE

Major: Accounting

Elected to Beta Gamma Sigma, 1956

Charter Member of Beta Alpha Psi, Alpha Omega Chapter, 1955

Meritorious Service Award from Alpha Omega Chapter, April 2, 1991

MAJOR RESEARCH PROJECTS

Monetary Unit Sampling — Researching and developing a new monetary unit sampling method, using the Moment Bound — with Dr. William L. Felix of the University of Arizona, and Dr. Richard Grimlund of the University of Iowa and Frank Koster of Arthur Andersen — 1985–1988.

A-Score — Researching and developing a new financial analysis multiple discriminate analysis model — with Dr. Edward I. Altman of New York University — 1979–1983.

Transaction Flow Auditing — Researching and developing, as chairman of the development task force, a new audit methodology based on risk assessment and focusing on internal control — with other firm personnel, 1973–1977 — Implementation in 1977.

PROFESSIONAL BACKGROUND

Active with standard setting activities and industry associations. Some of these are summarized below:

Current:
- Advisory Board Member of the Gabelli School of Business, Graduate and Undergraduate, Fordham University
- Chairman of the Audit Committee of the Goodnow Flow Association, Inc.

Prior:
- Member of the Advisory Board to the SEC and Financial Reporting Institute of the Leventhal School of Accounting, University of Southern California – 1993 to 2014
- Member of the Leventhal International Symposium on Audit Research Planning Committee – 1993 to 2015
- Member of the Consultative Advisory Group to the International Auditing and Assurance Standards Board of the International Federation of Accountants – 2000 through 2011
- Member of the Professional Advocacy Committee of the Information Systems Audit and Control Association (ISACA)

- Chairman of the International Auditing and Assurance Standards Board (previously designated as the International Auditing Practices Committee) of the International Federation of Accountants
- Member of the AICPA Auditing Standards Board
- Member of the AICPA International Strategy Committee
- Member of the International Auditing Standards Subcommittee of the Auditing Standards Board of the AICPA
- Chairman of the AICPA EDP Auditing Standards Subcommittee
- International President and Chairman of the International Board of Directors of the Information Systems, Audit and Control Association (ISACA) and the IT Governance Institute
- Member of the Governance Advisory Board of ISACA
- Member of the Audit Committee of ISACA
- Member of the Standards Board of ISACA
- Member of the International Federation of Accountants Subcommittee on Auditing in a Computer Environment
- Member of the AICPA Special Advisory Committee on Internal Control in the Federal Government
- Vice Chairman, Practice, of the Auditing Section of the American Accounting Association
- Member of AICPA Management Consulting Service Practice Standards and Administration Committee
- Member of the Publication Committee of the American Accounting Association
- Member of the Board of Research Advisors of the Institute of Internal Auditors

- Chairman of the Professional Publications Committee, American Accounting Association - Auditing Section
- Member of the AICPA Statistical Sampling Committee
- Member of the AICPA Reporting on Internal Controls Task Force
- Member of the EDP Auditors Foundation Research Advisory Committee
- Member of the New York State Society Auditing Standards and Procedures Committee
- Member of the AICPA Research Advisory Group
- Member of the Strategic Advisory Group of ISACA
- Member of the AAA Auditing Section's Distinguished Service Award in Auditing Committee (2007, as well as in 2006) — Invited to attend the two U.S. Department of Commerce, National Bureau of Standards Invitational Workshops sponsored to explore the subject of "Audit and Evaluation of Computer Security."

PUBLICATIONS

Corporate Governance in Italy, The Board of Auditors, Consiglio Nazionale Dottori Commercialisti, Rome, Italy, Fall 2003, co-editor

"The New Corporate Governance Model: A Focus on Independence, the Audit Committee and the Accounting Profession," the Marshall Magazine, Spring 2003

"A Case for Global Corporate Governance Rules: An Auditor's Perspective," International Journal of Auditing, pp. 203–211, Volume 4, Number 3, November 2000
> Reprinted in:
> Internal Control, ABG Professional Information, Issue 39, March 2001, London, England
> Corporate Governance, FTMS Consultants (S) Ptd Ltd, Issue 3, Volume 4, June 2001, Singapore
> Tolley's Corporate Governance Handbook, Reed Elsevier (UK) Ltd, 2002 and 2006

"The Development of International Standards on Auditing," The CPA Journal, pp. 14–20, October 1999

"Toward Better Financial Management and Reporting: A Discussion and a Challenge," Il Controllo Legale dei Conti, Milan, Italy, October 1999

"International Auditing: Reporting on the Credibility of Information," The Auditor's Report, Auditing Section, American Accounting Association, Vol., 21, No. 1, Fall, 1997.

"Adopting the International Standards on Auditing: An Opportunity and a Responsibility," IFAC Quarterly, Volume 20, Number 4, pp. 8–9, April 1997.

"International Auditing - Update," The <u>Auditor's Report</u>, Auditing Section, American Accounting Association, Vol., 19, No. 3, Summer 1996, pp. 7 & 9.

"New Focus for the International Standards on Auditing," <u>The Journal of International Accounting Auditing & Taxation</u>, Vol. 5, No. 1, 1996, pp. 133–146.

"Auditing Beyond 2000," IFAC <u>Quarterly</u>, Volume 19, No. 3, September 1995, pp. 11–13.

"The Changing World of International Accounting and Auditing," <u>Internal Auditor</u>, (April 1994), pp. 54–56.

"Developing International Accounting and Auditing Standards for World Markets," <u>Journal of International Accounting Auditing & Taxation</u>, A JAI Press, Inc. Publication, Volume 1, No. 1 (1992), pp. 1–11.

"Auditing Environmental Liabilities," <u>Auditing: A Journal of Practice & Theory</u>, Volume 11, No. 1 (Spring 1992), pp. 47–57.

"Definitions of Six Consulting Functions," (with Roger E. Muns and William E. Whitmer), <u>Journal of Accountancy</u>, (November 1991), pp. 43–45.

"Arthur Andersen's New Monetary Unit Sampling Approach," (with William L. Felix, Jr., Richard A. Grimlund, and Frank J. Koster), <u>Auditing: A Journal of Practice & Theory</u>, Volume 9, No. 3 (Fall, 1990), pp. 1–16.

"Subject Matter of Auditing," (with Edward J. Blocher and Bart H. Ward) in <u>Research Opportunities in Auditing: The Second Decade</u>, edited by A. Rashad Abdel-Khalik and Ira Solomon, (Sarasota: American Accounting Association, Auditing Section, 1988).

"Three New SASs: Closing the Communications Gap," (with Ernest L. Ten Eyke and Mimi Blanco-Best), <u>Journal of Accountancy</u>, (December 1988), pp. 44–52.

"The Auditor: Using the Microcomputer Today," <u>Internal Auditing</u>, A Warren, Gorham & Lamont Publication, (Winter 1987), pp. 12-18.

"The CPA in the Information Age: Today and Tomorrow," <u>Journal of Accountancy</u>, (October 1986), pp. 94-107.

"An Incorrect Rejection Problem in Monetary Unit Sampling," (with David Burgstahler and William L. Felix, Jr.) in <u>Auditing Research Symposium</u> edited by Richard E. Ziegler and Frederick L. Neumann, (Urbana/Champaign: University Press, University of Illinois, 1986).

"Statistical Inference and the IRS," (with William L. Felix, Jr.), <u>Journal of Accountancy</u>, (June 1985), pp. 38-45.

"Microcomputers and the Auditor," Journal of Accountancy, (December 1983), pp. 106-108.

"Microcomputers and the Auditor," The Auditor's Report, Auditing Section/American Accounting Association, Volume 7, No. 1 (Winter, 1983), pp. 1-2.

"Distributed Auditing in the DDP Environment," CA Magazine, (Canadian Institute of Chartered Accountants), (January 1982), pp. 86–88.

"Distributed Auditing in the Distributed Systems Environment," in EDP Audit Symposium 1981/82 Proceedings edited by Joseph L. Sardinas, Jr. (Amherst: Business Publications, University of Massachusetts, 1981).

"Auditing in a Computer Environment? The Integration of the Manual and EDP Portions of the Audit," in EDP Audit Symposium 1979/80 Proceedings edited by Joseph L. Sardinas, Jr. (Amherst: Business Publications, University of Massachusetts, 1980).

"To Blow the Whistle or Not: An Employee's Dilemma with Internal Control Implications," discussant's paper in Symposium on Auditing Research III (Urbana/Champaign: University Press, University of Illinois, 1978)

"Third-Party Review of the Computer Service Center," Journal of Accountancy, (August 1978), pp. 78–82.

"Audex 100 - A Computer Audit Program for Larger Memory Systems," The Arthur Andersen Chronicle, Volume 35, No. 3, (July 1975), pp. 10–18

"The Certified Public Accountant in Japan," The Arthur Andersen Chronicle, Volume 28, No. 3 (June 1968), pp. 8–11.

AWARDS

Joseph J. Wasserman Award, June 2017, the Metropolitan Chapter of the Information Systems Audit and Control Association (ISACA), recognizes Outstanding Achievement and Contribution to the Information Systems Audit, Control, Security, Risk Management, and/or Governance professions.

Sustained Contribution Award, October 2011, the American Institute of Certified Public Accountants, presented this inaugural award to 51 CPAs who have been recognized for their long-term service and leadership in the profession. All of the recipients have served on Institute volunteer groups for 20 or more years and have served at least once as a chair of an AICPA committee, task force or resource panel.

Eugene M. Frank Award for Meritorious Service, presented July 2007, by the Information Systems Audit and Control Association, at its International Conference in Singapore; the award given to individuals for "Many Years of Outstanding Service to ISACA."

Special Recognition Award, December 2004, the American Institute of Certified Public Accountants, presented at the Institute's Annual

SEC and PCAOB Conference in Washington, DC. The award is given only intermittently for significant contributions to the accounting profession. The award was presented to Robert Roussey for working tirelessly on establishing the credibility and recognition of the International Standards on Auditing, and for helping to bring them to world-class status, where the standards are being accepted and used in many countries around the world.

Distinguished Service in Auditing Award, June 1998, the Auditing Section of the American Accounting Association, presented at the Section's Annual Luncheon during the Annual Meeting of the Association, New Orleans, LA

Joint AICPA/AAA Collaboration Award, November 1998, of the Joint AICPA/AA Collaboration Award Committee, for participation in the Award-winning collaborative effort between academics and practitioners for the work entitled *Auditing Practice Research, and Education - A Productive Collaboration*

Meritorious Service Award, in *recognition of outstanding service to accounting education, the accounting profession and Beta Alpha Psi*, April 2, 1991, presented by the Alpha Omega Chapter at Fordham University of Beta Alpha Psi

EDITORIAL AND ADVISORY BOARDS

Board	Publication
Editorial Consulting Board	- Handbook of Corporate Finance, 1986
Editorial Consulting Board	- Handbook of Financial Markets & Institutions, 1987
Editorial Board	- Advances in Accounting, 1987–
Editorial Board	- Journal of International Accounting, Auditing and Taxation, 1991–
Editorial Board	- Auditing: A Journal of Practice & Theory, 1993–2002
Advisory Board	- International Journal of Auditing, 1995–2000
Advisory Board	- Fordham University, Graduate School of Business and the College of Business Administration (1999–2006)

REFERENCES

Who's Who in the Midwest - 1990–1991 Edition

Who's Who in the World - 1991–92 Edition and all subsequent editions

Who's Who in America - Current Editions since 1993

Who's Who in the West - Current Editions since 1994

DELEGATIONS

Electronic Data Processing the People's Republic of China
and Auditing Delegation and Hong Kong, April 25–May 16, 1986

SPEECHES 1980 - 2013	
Background on the development of the Accounting Profession in the U.S., International Accounting Standards and Future Issues	Chinese Institute of CPA delegation to the U.S., November 2012
Issues for the Accounting Profession in the U.S., International Accounting Standards and Future Issues	Chinese Institute of CPA delegation to the U.S. to study accounting issues and regulation, November 2011
The Changing Focus of Corporate Governance and IT Governance	Scandinavian ISACA Conference, Allborg Denmark, April 22, 2009
Current Issues in Accounting	USC Marshall School of Business and Leventhal School of Accounting, First Annual Reunion for Graduate Students, Los Angeles, April 3-5, 2009
Governance: A Focus on IT Governance, Security Governance and Valuation Governance	Institute of Internal Auditors, International Conference, 9 July 2007, Amsterdam
The Future of the Financial Statement Audit	Presenter and Moderator, Plenary Session, International Symposium on Auditing, Shanghai Jiao Tong University, 22 June 2007
IT Governance: An Important Part of Developing an Entity's Business and Organizational Strategies	Master of Accounting and Doctorial Students at Xiamen University, 18 June 2007, Xiamen, China
Vision Paper of the Six CEO's of the Largest International Network Accounting Firms on: Financial Reporting and Audit/Assurance Reporting and Regulation	Presenter and Moderator of the Vision Paper Discussion Panel, SEC and Financial Reporting Institute Annual Conference, University of Southern California, 31 May 2007
Assessing France's Joint Audit Requirement: Are Two Heads Better than One?	Discussant, International Symposium on Auditing, International Symposium on Auditing, University of New South Wales, 22 June 2006
The Auditor's Role in IT Governance	Information Systems Audit & Control Association, Singapore Chapter, 1 July, 2005
Oversight of Audit and Reporting Quality Across International Borders	International Symposium on Audit Research, Singapore, 30 June, 2005
IT Governance	Marshall School – ICIIP Executive Briefing on Risk Management, IT Governance and Information Security, Davidson Conference Center, 13 Oct 2004
IT Governance and Sarbanes-Oxley	XVII National Information Systems Auditing Conference, Cortona, Italy, 19 May 2004

Panel Presentation on Alternative Perspectives on Globalization	International Relations Undergraduate Association, 30 March 2004, USC
Going Forward: A Perspective on the Status and Future of the Accounting Profession	International Symposium on Audit Research, Los Angeles, CA, 30-31 May 2003
The New Business Model and IT Governance	Federation des Experts Compatables Europeaneens, Bucharest, 28-29 May 2003
Integrating Corporate Governance Across the Accounting Curriculum	Federation of Schools of Accountancy, Faculty Consortium, Chicago, 16-17 May 2003
Membership Update	Information Systems Audit and Control Association, Los Angeles Chapter April 2003
IT – In the New Business Model and IT Governance: What Accountants Need to Know	World Congress of Accountants, Hong Kong, November 18, 2002
IT Governance: An Important Aspect of Corporate Governance	Information Systems Audit and Control Association, Hong Kong Chapter, November 20, 2002
IT Governance: An Important Aspect of Corporate Governance	Conference: ISACA Denmark, Danish State Authorized Public Accountants, IIA Denmark and Association of Security Specialists, Copenhagen, Denmark, November 1, 2002
Corporate Governance and IT Security	Copenhagen Business School, Copenhagen, Denmark, November 1, 2002
The Changing Role of the Board of Directors and the Audit Committee in the United States	Conference on the "Effectiveness of Corporate Audits and the Financial Markets Crisis: The role of the Collegio Sindacale," Rome, Italy, October 11, 2002
Globalization of Standards: A Focus on International Standards on Auditing	Morison International – Joint Conference, San Jose, Costa Rica, July 25, 2002
The IT Profession in the New Millennium	Global Leadership Conference, ISACA International Conference, New York, NY July 6, 2002
IT Governance: An Important Topic for Boards of Directors, Management and Auditors	Joint Meeting of LA Chapters of the Information Systems Audit and Control Association and the Institute of Internal Auditors, Los Angeles, CA March 21, 2002
Information Systems Auditing and IT Governance	The Consultative Advisory Group meeting with the International Auditing and Assurance Standards Board, Madrid, Spain, December 14, 2001
Goals and Vision: Acceptance of the Presidency of the Information Systems Audit and Control Association	Annual General Meeting, Paris, France, June 11, 2001
Corporate Governance in the International Environment	The International Symposium on Auditing Research, Maastricht University, July 2000

Status and Progress of the International Auditing Practices Committee	Report to the Council of the International Federation of Accountants, Edinburgh, Scotland, May 2000
International Standards on Auditing: Strategy and Direction	Conference of the Chamber of Auditors of the Czech Republic, Prague, March 2000
Strategy and Programs of the International Auditing Practices Committee	Annual meeting of the Consultative Advisory Group, Paris, France, November 18-19, 1999
Audit Risk & Quality in the International Environment	The International Symposium on Auditing Research, University of Southern California, Redondo Beach, California, June 25, 1999
International Standards on Auditing	Meeting of the Cal Society, Accounting Principles & Auditing Standards Committee, Monterey, California, May 20, 1999
International Accounting & Auditing Standards in Practice	The UIUC-34th International Accounting Conference, University of Illinois, Champaign-Urbana, April 22-24, 1999
International Standards on Auditing: Strategy and Direction	Conference of the Collegi de Censors Jurats de Comptes de Catalunya, Barcelona, Spain, March 4, 1999
Globalization of Accounting and Business in the Accounting Curriculum	The Accounting Forum, University of Southern California, February 5, 1999
Strategies of the International Auditing Practices Committee	Annual meeting of the Consultative Advisory Committee, Amsterdam, The Netherlands, November 19-20, 1998
Challenges of the Accountancy Profession in the World of Diversified Social and Economic Development	50th Anniversary Celebration, International Symposium, Japanese Institute of CPAs, Tokyo, Japan, October 23, 1998
Globalization of Accounting and Auditing	Annual meeting of the CMA Society of Southern California, San Marcos Country Club, San Diego, CA, September 12, 1998
International Standards on Auditing: Strategy and Direction, and Auditing Derivatives	Seminar of the Federacion de Colegios de Contradores Publicos de Venezuela, Caracas, Venezuela, June 16, 1998

The International Standards on Auditing	Conference on International Auditing, sponsored by the Consiglio Nazionale dei Dottori Commercialisti, and the Consiglio Nazionale dei Ragioniere (the two Accountancy bodies in Italy), Rome, Italy, March 5, 1998
Global Direction & Issues: Focus on Auditing	Seminar for Students from Monash University, Australia, University of Southern California, Los Angeles, February 4, 1998
Auditing Standards: Direction & Issues	Mid-Year Conference, Auditing Section, American Accounting Association, Plenary session Speaker, Mesa, Arizona, January 23, 1998
The International Auditing Standards: Use in the Global Capital Markets by the Accountancy Profession	Meeting of the Professional Standards and Regulations Committee of the Arthur Andersen Worldwide Organization, Brussels, Belgium, July 31, 1997
Corporate Governance: A Case for Global Rules	Plenary Session, The International Symposium on Audit Research, Singapore, July 26, 1997
Global Financing: The Role of the Accountancy Profession	The ASEAN Federation of Accountants Lecture of the Year, Singapore, June 25, 1997
Future Direction of Auditing Standards and the Expectation Gap	Auditing Seminar, The Fiji Institute of Accountants, Fiji, June 17, 1997
Report on the Achievements and Plans of the International Auditing Practices Committee for 1997-97	Meeting of Council of the International Federation of Accountants, Santo Domingo, May 9, 1997
Future Direction of Auditing Standards and the Expectation Gap	Auditing Seminar, The Malta Institute of Accountants, March 4, 1997
The Role of the International Auditing Practices Committee in Setting International Auditing Standards	Conference on the Role, the Position and the Liability of the Statutory Auditor within the European Union, Commission of the European Commission of the European Communities, Brussels, Belgium, December 6, 1996
The State of International Auditing: 1996	The 6th Jerusalem Conference on Accountancy, Jerusalem, Israel, November 12, 1996
Future Direction of Auditing Standards and the Expectation Gap	Auditing Seminar, The Institute of Certified Public Accountants of Singapore, Singapore, October 29, 1996
Report on the Status of Endorsement of the International Standards on Auditing by the International Organization of Securities Commissions	Meeting of Council of the International Federation of Accountants, Kuala Lumpur, Malaysia, October 11, 1996
The Role, Position and Liability of the Statutory Auditor within the European Union	Plenary Session, Discussant, International Symposium on Auditing Research, Maastricht, The Netherlands, June 24, 1996
Views of the International Auditing Practices Committee on the Going Concern Assumption	International Accounting Standards Committee Board Meeting, Stockholm, Sweden, June 11, 1996

The Codification of International Standards on Auditing and Related Matters	Meeting of the Financial Reporting Working Party No. 1, Auditing Subgroup, of the International Organization of Securities Commissions, the Securities Exchange Commission, Washington, D.C. April 18, 1996
New International Auditor's Report	Financial Reporting Conference, Mexican Institute of Certified Public Accountants, Mexico City, June 23, 1995
Assurance Services in the 21st Century	International Accounting Conference, International Federation of Accountants and Federation Experts Comptables Europeens, Amsterdam, The Netherlands, May 12, 1995
The Auditor's Workplace of the Future	Western Intergovernmental Forum, Pasadena, CA, March 24, 1995
The New International Auditing Standard on the Auditor's Report	Israel Institute of Certified Public Accountants, International Auditing Seminar, Tel Aviv, Israel, March 6, 1995
Environmental Auditing Research Opportunities	American Accounting Association, Auditing Section, Mid-Year Meeting, Las Vegas, Nevada, February 20, 1995
Audit Research and Future Developments in the Profession	The International Federation of Accountants Conference of Audit Standard-Setting Bodies, June 27-28, 1994, Paris, France
The Implications of SAS No. 65 to the External and Internal Auditor	The Institute of Internal Auditors 51st Annual Conference, Phoenix, Arizona, June 23, 1992
Internal Control Issues	Hawaiian Society of CPAs, Annual Professional Development Conference, Honolulu, Hawaii, May 21, 1992
Impact of Research on Practice	American Accounting Association Western Regional Meeting, San Jose, CA, May 1, 1992
Implications of SAS No. 65 to the External and Internal Auditor	The Institute of Internal Auditors, Central Illinois Chapter, Champaign, IL, April 15, 1992
Standard Setting in the Global Marketplace	J.L. Kellogg Graduate School of Management, Northwestern University, Evanston, IL, March 3, 1992
Discussant: The Research vs. Teaching Debate in Auditing	American Accounting Association/Price Waterhouse Conference on Audit Education, San Diego, CA, February 14-15, 1992
Impact of Audit Research on Practice	University of Southern California, Audit Judgment Symposium, Los Angeles, CA, February 17-18, 1992
Current Initiatives Dealing with Internal Control and their Implications	Arthur Andersen Accounting and Auditing Symposium for Faculty, St. Charles, IL, November 11, 1991

Accounting Education and Practice, Beyond the Year 2000: Meeting the Challenges	Third Asian-Pacific Conference on International Accounting Issues, Honolulu, Hawaii, October 16, 1991
Current Issues on Internal Controls, at a Technical Session, Presented by Members of the Internal Auditing Practices Committee of the International Federation of Accountants	XIX Inter-America Conference of Accountants, Buenos Aires, Argentina, October 9, 1991
Internal Control	Virginia CPA Society, Professional Development Conference, Reston, Virginia, September 6, 1991
The Auditors' Consideration of the Internal Audit Function in an Audit of Financial Statements, SAS No. 95	The Institute of Internal Auditors, Western Regional Conference, Denver, Colorado, August 19, 1991
Emerging Issues in International Accounting: Practitioners' Perspectives	American Accounting Association, Annual Meeting, Panel Session, Nashville, Tennessee, August 13, 1991
Developing International Auditing and Accounting Standards for World Markets	American Accounting Association, Annual Meeting, Luncheon Speech to the International Accounting Section, Nashville, Tennessee, August 12, 1991
Internal Controls: Developments that Could Dramatically Affect Education, Business and the Audit Profession	American Accounting Association, Annual Meeting, CPE Session, Nashville, Tennessee, August 11, 1991
Detection of Computer Fraud	Annual Illinois CPA Society, Professional Liability Conference, Oak Brook Marriott, IL, May 29, 1991
The Accounting Profession – Self Regulation: Is It Dead? and The Development of International Accounting and Auditing Standards	Beta Alpha Psi Business Day, Fordham University, NY, April 8, 1991
Environmental Liabilities in the 1990s	The Second Annual Critical Perspective Symposium: Ethics, Regulations, and Professionalism in Accounting; Public Interest Section, American Accounting Association, New York, NY, March 23-24, 1991
The Auditor's Consideration of the Internal Audit Function in an Audit of Financial Statements	Institute of Internal Auditors, Chicago Chapter, Chicago, IL, February 27, 1991
Discussant: Inherent Risk	Audit Judgment Symposium, University of Southern California, School of Accounting, February 18-19, 1991
Management Reporting on Internal Controls	Institute of Internal Auditors, Chicago Chapter, Chicago, IL, November 19, 1990
SAS No. 9 Update	Illinois CPA Foundation 1990 Internal Auditing Issues Conference, September 12, 1990
Auditing Standards Board Update and Emerging Issues	44th Annual Conference on Accountants, The University of Tulsa, Tulsa, Oklahoma, April 26, 1990
SAS No. 9 Update	Institute of Internal Auditors, New York Chapter, New York, NY, March 21, 1990
SAS No. 9 Update	Institute of Internal Auditors, Washington, D.C. Chapter, Washington, D.C. March 15, 1990

A Continuing Challenge: Advances in Audit Technology	18th Annual Fall Accounting Conference, Beta Alpha, Psi, University of South Florida, Tampa, FL, November 10, 1989
Effective Audit Committee Oversight	American Accounting Association, Annual Meeting, Honolulu, Hawaii, August 16, 1989
Advances in Audit Technology	Association of Government Accountants, Los Angeles, CA, June 27, 1989
Errors, Irregularities, and Illegal Acts	Midwestern Intergovernmental Audit Forum, Indianapolis, MD, May 10, 1989
The Auditing Standards Board – New Pronouncements and Current Issues	J.L. Kellogg Graduate School of Management, Northwestern University, Evenson, IL, February 23, 1989
Errors, Irregularities, and Illegal Acts	Mountain & Plains Intergovernmental Audit Forum, Denver, Colorado, December 8, 1988
Implementing the New ASB Pronouncements	Accounting & Audit Faculty Symposium, Arthur Andersen & Co., St. Charles, IL, October 17, 1988
The SEC Proposal on Management Reporting	Financial Executives Institute, Chicago Loop Chapter, Chicago, IL, September 8, 1988
Implementing the New ASB Pronouncement, Panel Session: New Pronouncements	AICPA National Accounting & Auditing Advanced Technical Symposium, Washington, D.C., June 14, 1988
Implementing the New ASB Pronouncements	J.L. Kellogg Graduate School of Management, Northwestern University, Evanston, IL, May 19, 1988
Current Developments in Auditing Standards	1988 Kansas Society of CPAs Municipal Accounting Seminar, May 18, 1988
Workpaper Evolution – Present and Future	Illinois CPA Foundation, 1988 Automated Workpaper Conference, May 12, 1988
The Auditing Standards Board: The Expectation Gap Statements and Current Developments	National Association of Accountants Ohio Council, 14th Annual Professional Development Conference, Kent State University, April 27-28, 1988
The New Standard Auditor's Report and the Other Expectation Gap Statements on Auditing Standards	University of Arizona, April 18, 1988
Trends in Information Technology	EDP Auditors Association, International Conference on Computer Audit, Control and Security, Atlanta, GA, April 11, 1988
Discussant: The Impact of Technology on Auditing in the Year 2000, and The Role of ES in the Audit or Large Data Base Systems	Audit Judgment Symposium, University of Southern California, School of Accounting, Center of Accounting Research, Los Angeles, CA, February 15-16, 1988
Use of the Microcomputer in Auditing	Institute of Internal Auditors, Chicago West Chapter, February 2, 1988
10 ASB Exposure Drafts	FEI Conference, New York, NY, November 9, 1987
Automating the Auditor and Perspectives on China's Use of Computer Technology	EDPAA Milwaukee Presentations, September 10, 1986

Automating the Auditor	EDP Auditors Association, 14th International Conference, Miami, FL, June 23-25, 1986
Microcomputer Trends 1981-1990 and History of Auditing in the United States	Presentations in China, May, 1986
Automating the Auditor	University of Hawaii, Accounting Club and Beta Alpha Psi Accounting: A Glimpse into the Future, January 10, 1986
Automating the Auditor	Automated Audit Symposium & Software Exchange, Las Vegas, NV, November 19, 1985
Automating the Auditor	Illinois State University, Normal, IL, October 16, 1985
The Computer and the Accountant	Nebraska Society of Certified Public Accountants Mid-America Accounting & Auditing Conference, Lincoln, NB, September 9-10, 1985
Automating the Auditor	Association of Government Accountants, 34th Annual Professional Development Conference, San Diego, CA, June 24-25, 1985
Automating the Auditor	Midwest American Accounting Association Meeting, Chicago, IL, March 27-29, 1985
Automating the Auditor	EDP Auditors Association & Institute of Internal Auditors, Microcomputer Audit, Control, & Security Conference, Houston, TX, December 3-5, 1984
Computer Security in Practice	DOD/NBS – 7th Annual Conference on Computer Security, Washington, D.C., September 24-26-1984
Automating the Auditor	The Institute of Internal Auditors, International Conference, Chicago, IL, June 17, 1984
Microcomputers in Business	American Accounting Association, New Orleans, LA, August 22, 1983
Auditing in the 80's & Emerging Issues	University of Denver, School of Accounting Professional Standards Accounting Seminar, April 20, 1983
Extent of Testing in Auditing	University of Georgia – Center for Audit Research, March 22-23, 1983
Controls and Risks in the Microcomputer or Small Business Computer Environment	Institute of Internal Auditors, Toledo Chapter, Toledo, OH, September 14, 1981
Discussant: A New Framework for Predicting Firms in Financial Distress	American Accounting Association Annual Meeting, Chicago, IL, August 5, 1981
Control Standards in a Microenvironment	The Institute of Internal Auditors 40th International Conference, Phoenix, AZ, June 7-10, 1981
Auditing in a Computer Environment	Office of the Inspector General, Computer Seminar, FBI Academy, Quantico, VA, February 13, 1981
Public Accountability and the Acquisition Process-Fiscal and Operational Accountability: A Private Sector View	National Contract Management Association, 17th Annual Educational Symposium, Los Angeles, CA, November 13, 1980
Focus on Audit/Control in Computer Environments-Control Considerations in the Private Sector	

CLUBS, PROFESSIONAL SOCIETIES AND OTHER ORGANIZATIONAL MEMBERSHIPS

Beta Gamma Sigma	National Honor Fraternity	Present
Beta Gamma Sigma Alumni in New York City	Social Fraternity	Past
Beta Alpha Psi Alpha Omega Chapter at Fordham University	Accounting Honor Fraternity Fordham Chapter	Past
Accounting Society of Fordham University	Academic	Past
New York State Association of CPA Candidates	Professional Society	Past (1)
New York State Society of Certified Public Accountants	Professional Society	Present (2)
American Institute of Certified Public Accountants	Professional Society	Present (2)
Japanese Institute of Certified Public Accountants	Professional Society	Prior
The Illinois Society of Certified Public Accountants	Professional Society	Past
The American Chamber of Commerce in Japan	Civic Organization	Past (2)
The American-Japan Society, Tokyo, Japan	Civic Organization	Past
Beaver Creek Club	Social/Golf and Ski	Current
The Hammock Dunes Club	Social/Golf	Current
The Japan Society, New York	Civic Organization	Past
Fort Hill Island Country Club, New Rochelle, New York	Social	Past
Tokyo American Club	Social	Present (Life Member)
St. Joseph's Mems Club, Bronxville, New York	Church	Past (3)
United Fund of Eastchester/Bronxville, New York	Civic	Past (4)
The Metropolitan Club, New York	Business/Social	Present (5)
The Union League Club of Chicago	Business/Social	Prior
Boy Scouts of America, Troop No. 13, Kenilworth, IL	Educational	Past (3)
Scarsdale Golf Club, Scarsdale, NY	Social/Golf	Past

Goodnow Flow Association	Recreational	Present (2)
Fordham University, President Club Committee, Advisory Board, Graduate School of Business	Civic/Philanthropic Civic	Past (4) Past (2)
Kenilworth Club, Kenilworth, IL.	Social	Past
Kenilworth Community House, Kenilworth, IL,	Civic	Past (6)
The Information Systems Audit and Control Association (ISACA)	Business/Philanthropic, Educational	Present (1, 2, 6)
The Institute of Internal Auditors	Business	Past (2)
International Federation of Accountants, New York	Professional Institute Society	Past (2)

Served As:

(1) President

(2) Committee Member, Committee Chairman, Etc.

(3) Director, Treasurer

(4) Fund Raiser, Committee Member

(5) Member of Board of Governors, Chairman of Finance Committee

(6) Director